THE COMPLETE
KODAK ANIMATION BOOK

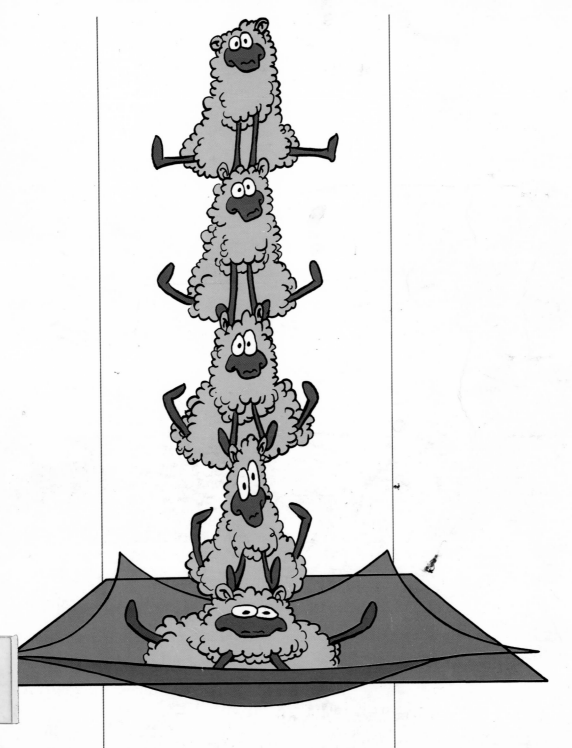

THE COMPLETE KODAK ANIMATION BOOK

Eastman Kodak Company
Rochester, New York 14650

The Authors

A SALUTE TO THE CREATORS

This book recognizes the talented men and women, from yesterday and today, who have made a creative contribution to the film industry. It is our hope that these people will serve as an example to inspire others to achieve their creative best with Eastman film.

Library of Congress Catalog Card No. 83-88895

ISBN 0-87985-330-1

Library of Congress Cataloging in Publication Data

Solomon, Charles.
   The complete Kodak animation book.

   Bibliography: p.
   Includes index.
   Summary: A survey of animation, its history, techniques, animators of the past and present, careers, and how to do it yourself.
   1. Animation (Cinematography) (1. Animation [Cinematography]) I. Stark, Ron. II. Eastman Kodak Company. III. Title.
TR897.5.S64   1983   778.5′347   83-88895
ISBN 0-87985-330-1

Cover and book design: Bill Buckett Associates, Inc.
Cover animation: © SHEEP BOUNCE, David Silverman

Printed in the United States of America

10 9 8 7 6 5 4 3 2 1

An MFA candidate in film at UCLA, Charles Solomon is a member of the board of the International Animated Film Society/ASIFA-Hollywood. His writings about animation have appeared in the *Los Angeles Times, Rolling Stone, Film Comment, Millimeter, Crawdaddy,* and *Graffiti,* and have been reprinted in more than three dozen newspapers and professional journals in the United States, Canada, and France. He was selected for the international jury of the Ottawa Animation Festival in 1982 and does animation programming for the Academy of Motion Picture Arts and Sciences. After receiving an MA in cultural history, Solomon did research in animation history under a grant from the Swann Foundation, and continues to work with ASIFA and UCLA archives.

Ron Stark is an accomplished commercial producer, director, and voice actor. He is a vice-president of the International Animated Film Society/ASIFA-Hollywood and creator and administrator of their animation art conservation program. He is recognized internationally as a leading authority on animation art restoration. He is also a member of the Los Angeles Society for Paint and Coatings Technology, the Western Association for Art Conservation, and the Directors Guild of America.

Acknowledgements

Producing a book of this nature requires the help of many people. Special thanks for special help are due to our editor, Jackie Salitan, for patience and enthusiasm in the face of changes, problems, deadlines, and other crises; Bob Kurtz, Shelly Kurtz-Regaldo, and Lorraine Roberts at Kurtz and Friends; Jack Lindquist, David Pacheco, Howard Green, Bob Gibeaut, Dave Smith, Paula Sigman, and Vince Jefferds at Walt Disney Productions; Bill Hanna, Joe Barbera, Art Scott, Harry Love, Iwao Takamoto, John Michaeli, and Sarah Baisley at Hanna-Barbera Productions; Hal Geer and Friz Freleng at Warner Brothers; Chuck Jones and Marion Dern; Bill Scott, John Halas, Prescott Wright, and Darr Hawthorne; Dan McLaughlin and Robert Rosen at UCLA; Eric Timmerman at RIT; Nick, Tee, and the late Stephen Bosustow of Bosustow Productions; Elfriede Fischinger and William Moritz; Patty van Hinckeldy at Will Vinton Productions; Lorraine Good and Anabelle Winship of the Film Canada Center; Ann Garneau at the National Film Board of Canada; Louise Beaudet at the Cinematique Quebecoise; Allan Bobey and Phil Condax at the International Museum of Photography, George Eastman House; Richard Taylor and Craig Reynolds; Chia Gary Wang for his help with translation; George Gardner and Paul Tokarski for their camera work; Mark Kausler; Hans Bacher, Ed Herscovitz, Yoram Gross, Marcell Jankovics, Raoul Servais, Frederic Back, Jannick Hastrup, Anatoly Dyuzhev, and Italtoons for assistance on the international chapter; the Academy of Motion Picture Arts and Sciences for their library and staff assistance; the Los Angeles Society for Coating Technology for technical assistance; Juliann Stark, Peter Daniels and staff, George McIntyre, Rose Solomon, Ann Solomon, Marvin and Marsha Francis, Sophocles W. Bunce, Lewis Segal, Hank Cato, David Silverman, Gary Campbell, Anne Pautler, Stephen Ainsworth, and Kevin Caffey for creative input and support. Additional thanks are due to all the artists who contributed their time and knowledge in interviews and their talents in illustrations.

—CHARLES SOLOMON AND RON STARK

"Figment" (right), drawn by Bob Kurtz and David Pacheco, is a "real life" audioanimatronic character created by Walt Disney Productions for the Kodak Showcase "Journey Into Imagination," at the Walt Disney World Epcot Center near Orlando, Florida. The Kodak Showcase features numerous creative uses of film, including the first-time-ever use of 3-D computer-generated animation interwoven with live-action photography in the 3-D film *Magic Journeys*.

Table of Contents

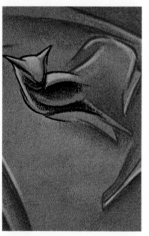

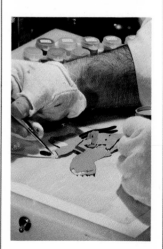

Introduction

Welcome to the world of animation, a world that stretches to the limits of human imagination and whose heart lies deep in mankind's desire to create.

The dictionary explains that "animation" is derived from *anima,* the Latin word for soul or spirit; that the verb "to animate" literally means "to give life to:" that the term is used to describe a variety of frame-by-frame film-making techniques. While this definition is adequate, it fails to capture the essence of animation, just as a textbook on optics fails to convey the feeling of moonlight.

Animation can be magic.

Animation can make an audience roar with laughter as a hapless coyote falls off a cliff for the umpteenth time, and make the same audience weep at the plight of a lonely little elephant, separated from his mother. It may be the most powerful tool for communication ever devised, one that can transcend cultural and linguistic boundaries.

Animation may be a collective studio effort by hundreds of men and women or the unique expression of an individual artist's ideas and talents—a personal statement as intimate as a poem.

Animation may be macroscopic or microscopic: the turning of galaxies hundreds of light-years across and the infinitesmal movements of subatomic particles can be created with equal facility.

To the casual observer, animation may seem miraculous. How else could a few lines on a piece of paper or a small puppet of rubber and fur become a living personality, a character whose thoughts and feelings can be understood by an audience? But an animated film is no more miraculous than a painting, a novel, a symphony or a ballet. Each begins as an idea in a human mind; each requires enormous amounts of thought, time, creativity, labor, and love to become a reality. For beyond the dancing bunnies and the mice with sticks of dynamite lies another part of the world of animation.

Animation is also a college student turning down an invitation to a party so that he can redo 60 drawings for the fourth time because the movement still isn't perfect; a camera operator adjusting a piece of artwork in increments of a few thousandths of an inch; an independent artist sighing as she picks up the 534th drawing in a sequence and begins to shade it with colored pencils, knowing there are 1,466 more to do; a computer programmer studying a pattern of dots on a video monitor; a tired writer trying to think of a hilarious gag for a cartoon character—at 4:00 o'clock on a rainy Friday afternoon; a painter, her brush gliding over the surface of a cel like an ice skater, carefully making sure that the paint is covering the correct area evenly; a director, staring at a stop watch, trying to decide whether a character should look shocked for 10/24ths of a second or 11/24ths of a second.

The world of animation encompasses myriad techniques, styles and individuals: the only limits to the medium are the ones a filmmaker cares to impose. After 76 years, artists have only begun to explore the potential of animation. This book is intended to provide an overview of that exploration. You'll read about the films, the people who create them and the techniques they employ.

To the world of animation, the most flexible, protean, and challenging art form mankind has devised, Welcome.

1

A Short History of Studio Animation

It has become commonplace to begin histories of animation with descriptions of animals with extra sets of legs painted on the walls of caves in northern Spain some 30,000 years ago, or the sequential paintings of actions in Egyptian tombs or on Greek vases. While these works undoubtedly represent a manifestation of the spirit that led to the creation of animated films—the desire of the artist to endow his or her creations with movement—they are ultimately dead ends. Animation, as we know it, derives from these paintings only in a vague, spiritual sense, as modern fashions are descended from garments of animal skins.

The real story of animation (and of all filmmaking) began in the 17th century with the invention of the magic lantern by Athanasius Kircher, a Jesuit priest. The magic lantern was little more than a metal box with a lamp inside. A lens covered a hole in one side. Light from the lamp passed through an image painted on a glass slide held just behind the lens and then through the lens to project the image. The technology of this "magic" toy rapidly grew more sophisticated, and by the end of the 17th century Johannes Zahn had demonstrated that glass slides mounted in a revolving disc could give an illusion of movement.

At the end of the 18th century, popular interest in the magic lantern was stimulated in France by its use in horrifying ghost shows. Using lanterns that could dissolve one image into another in register or show slides in sequence, macabre illustrations depicting skeletons and recently dead political figures were projected onto clouds of smoke, mirrors, sheets of cloth, and pieces of glass. Adjustments of the lenses could provide the phantasmagoric effect of a zoom. Audiences were terrified and delighted by the shows.

Athanasius Kircher, a Jesuit priest, began the real story of animation with his invention of the magic lantern (right) in the 17th century. By the end of the 18th century, the "toy" had evolved into a popular form of entertainment (left).

COURTESY OF BRIAN COE, CURATOR OF KODAK MUSEUM IN HARROW

Magic lanterns remained popular throughout the 19th century in Europe and America, although the subjects of the slides became less grotesque. A home market grew up for the lanterns and slides as a simple form of entertainment. In the opening of REMBRANCE OF THINGS PAST, Marcel Proust describes a magic lantern producing phantoms of light that moved over the walls of his bedroom when his great aunt presented shows depicting scenes from medieval French history.

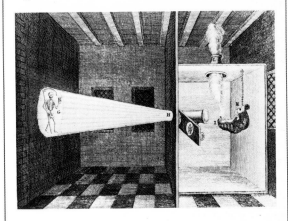

The magic lantern also retained its place in public entertainment. Music hall, variety, and vaudeville shows featured magicians who used the familiar elements—smoke, mirrors, glass, and lantern projections—to produce "magic" and illusions. A fascination with illusions of light and movement runs through 19th century western culture. The magic lantern shows are but a single example. Panoramas and dioramas that involved huge paintings, lights, and shifting viewpoints enjoyed an enormous popularity, as did shadow shows or "ombres chinoises."

It was in this atmosphere that Peter Roget published his *Persistence of Vision with Regard to Moving Objects* in 1824. Although some parts of this work have subsequently been proved inaccurate, the concept that the eye will merge still images together if they are presented rapidly enough and with a sufficient amount of light greatly influenced the development of motion pictures.

Roget's work led to a flood of experimentation and invention that produced numerous animation or "philosophical" toys, which found a ready market in Europe and America. The phenakistiscope and the zoetrope used sequences of drawings that were spun and watched through slits. (The slits provided the interruptions needed for the eye to meld the images together—the same function performed by the shutter of a motion picture projector.) Also popular was the praxinoscope which used a similar circular strip of drawings that were reflected into a smaller circular set of mirrors and then viewed through a single opening. Another poular toy, the thaumatrope, consisted of a disc with an image painted on each side. When the disc was spun, the images seemed to be combined— the crown would appear on the king's head or the bird would appear in the cage. A favorite toy (and still popular) was the flip book, a sequence of drawings bound together that gave the illusion of movement when rapidly flipped.

Another manifestation of this fascination with illusions of light was the popularity of photography. The first photographs were taken during the 1820's and 30's. Credit for having taken the first photograph is still disputed between proponents of Nicéphore Niépce and Louis Daguerre. Photography quickly became

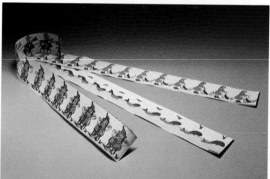

The zoetrope was just one of numerous animation or "philosophical" toys created in a spirit of experimentation and invention in the 19th century. Circular strips of drawings (center) were spun and watched through the slits to create the illusion of motion.

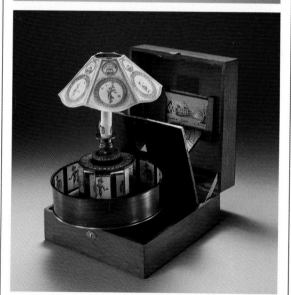

The praxinoscope, invented by Emile Reynaud in 1877, used strips of sequential images, similar to those for the zoetrope, but painted on clear, flexible strips. The images were reflected off mirrors and viewed from a specific point—in this case a slot in the lid of the box. In 1892, Reynaud caused a sensation when he set up a large praxinoscope, billed as the *Théâtre optique,* in the Musée Grevin and presented short plays to a musical accompaniment.

a widespread hobby and profession. Here was a way to use light to permanently fix an image from life. Now, if only motion could be captured as well . . .

Exactly when and where and by whom the first motion picture projections were made is also the subject of widespread debate, based on evidence that is fragmentary and inconclusive. But it is clear that the work of certain figures involved in the early experiments ultimately led to motion picture filmmaking as we know it. Eadweard Muybridge began experimenting with sequential photographs of race horses as early as 1873. Phenakistiscope discs and lantern slides were made from the photographs that resulted from a more successful series of studies of the gaits of horses in the years 1877–78. These studies culminated in his two folio sets of sequential photographs, *Animals in Motion* (1899) and *The Human Figure in Motion* (1901), which were later published in book form and remain standard references. This type of motion analysis was also practiced by the artist Thomas Eakins, who collaborated with Muybridge in 1884–85, and is used today by biologists and physiologists.

A device for recording sequential pictures was produced in Thomas Edison's laboratory in 1888. Edison wanted to supplement his recordings of voices and sounds with pictures. Curiously, he did not seem to have been particularly interested in projecting those pictures, but was content with reproducing them on cards which were shown on the mutoscope, a sort of mechanical flip book.

At this time, the light-sensitive emulsion was affixed to sheets of metal or glass on which a single exposure could be made. These plates made reloading a cumbersome operation and precluded effective sequential photography.

Roll film became available in 1888 through a process patented by George Eastman. The light, flexible celluloid base made it possible to keep enough film in the camera to take several photographs in succession without reloading. Then early in 1895 in Paris, the Lumiere brothers showed the first public motion picture projection and made it possible for a large audience to see a given set of images at the same time.

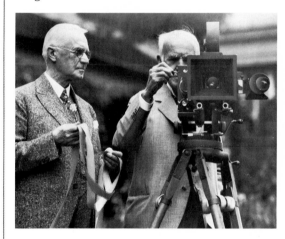

Magic lanterns, magician's tricks, animation toys, sequential photography, motion pictures: While these aspects of the popular interest in light and illusion seem quite disparate, J. Stuart Blackton linked them all. He toured with a magic act named Reader, Smith, and Blackton that used some of the old lantern tricks. Blackton, billed as the Komikal Kartoonist, did a chalk-talk routine. He also worked as a newspaper writer and illustrator. In April 1896, the *New York World* sent him to interview and sketch Thomas Edison. Edison, in return, shot a short film of Blackton doing a sketch entitled BLACKTON, THE EVENING WORLD CARTOONIST (1896).

Cartoonists at work had been used as subjects for the 1-minute short films that were shown in vaudeville houses and music halls. But Blackton seems to have been intrigued by the possibilities that filming a drawing in progress offered, although his main interest was in live-action filmmaking. With his partner, Albert E. Smith, Blackton helped found the Vitagraph Company, an early motion picture studio which eventually became Warner Brothers. When theatres clamored for footage of the naval encounters of the Spanish American War in 1899, Smith and Blackton faked some by using water, smoke, pinches of gunpowder, and cutouts attached to fine threads to produce one of the first examples of stop-motion animation with special effects. The film and lenses were so crude at that time that the "newsreel" was quite convincing.

At the turn of the century, Blackton returned to Edison's laboratory to make a "trik-film," THE ENCHANTED DRAWING, that involved chalk sketches of objects like cigars and bottles being replaced by the real items. Blackton actually appeared in this film at the chalkboard. In 1906, he went back to the chalkboard to create THE HUMOROUS PHASES OF FUNNY FACES, an animated chalk-talk that is generally considered to be the first animated film. Although he did several other pieces of animation, Blackton was too involved in the Vitagraph Company to devote much attention to animation, and the importance of his work went unrecognized during his lifetime.

Later in 1906, the French artist Emile Cohl began working on his Phantasmagorie series—the first animated series—involving white-on-black stick figures whom he christened les Fantouches (the Puppets). While Cohl's work retains a distinct charm today, his techniques were simple, even crude, when compared with the work of the greatest of the early animators, Winsor McCay.

Winsor McCay did not invent animation, as is sometimes claimed, but he was the first to demonstrate the artistic potential of the medium. A superb draftsman with an extraordinary ability to render in perspective, he quickly established himself as one of the finest comic-strip artists of all time. His most famous strip is the surreal "Little Nemo in Slumberland," which he began in 1905.

A Sunday panel from "Little Nemo in Slumberland" illustrates Winsor McCay's extraordinary draftsmanship. He subsequently used the characters from his popular comic strip in an animated film and an operetta with music by Victor Herbert.

October 22, 1905

3

Inspired by the flip books his son had cut out of the Sunday comic pages, McCay made his first film in 1911—a plotless series of encounters involving characters from LITTLE NEMO. He had each frame of the completed film hand-tinted, creating the first animation in color. McCay used this film in his vaudeville chalk-talk act, with less success than might be expected. Unfamiliar with the smoothness of his animation, audiences assumed he had made LITTLE NEMO and his next film, THE STORY OF A MOSQUITO, using photographs, models, and trick photography.

For the subject of his next film, McCay chose an animal that couldn't be faked. The result was GERTIE THE DINOSAUR (1914), which remains one of the seminal films in the history of animation. McCay made over 5,000 drawings for GERTIE THE DINOSAUR in India ink on rice paper; he allowed a neighbor boy, John Fitzsimmons, to retrace the background in each frame. The animation is fluid and elegant, with carefully timed movements drawn with McCay's usual sense of perspective. Even after more than 50 years of advances in technology and techniques, there are few contemporary films that can match GERTIE THE DINOSAUR for beauty of animation.

GERTIE was the first real example of character animation; she had a distinct, slightly childish, but appealing personality. McCay used segments of this film in his vaudeville act as well. GERTIE was timed to respond to his verbal commands—and received the popular recognition he had sought with NEMO and MOSQUITO. Audiences realized they were seeing something new: a film composed of drawings.

At about the same time, the first animation studios were founded in New York. Raoul Barré, who devised the first system of *pegs* for

An original drawing from GERTIE THE DINOSAUR (India ink on rice paper); McCay drew the figures himself, but had an assistant trace the background.

A scene from COLONEL HEEZA LIAR AND THE PIRATES (1916) from the J. R. Bray Studio: a typical example of the studio cartoons of that period.

A page from Max Fleischer's patent application for his rotoscope, a device that allowed animators to trace over live-action film to ensure realistic motion. The patent was granted in 1917.

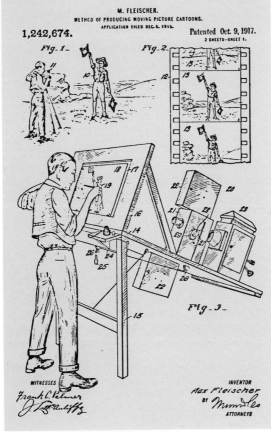

registering drawings, opened the first studio in 1913. J. R. Bray followed shortly after, and began producing a series of adventures about Colonel Heeza Liar, an animated caricature of Teddy Roosevelt. In 1915, Earl Hurd patented the technique of using clear celluloid sheets (cels) instead of paper, which freed animators from having to retrace the background for every drawing: The characters could be drawn on a separate level, with the background showing through the clear celluloid around them. Two years later, Bray and Hurd pooled their resources in the Bray-Hurd studio; they controlled the patents on most of the animation techniques then in use.

Max Fleischer, who worked with Bray as an apprentice, entered the animation business in 1915 when he filed for a patent on his rotoscope, a device that allowed animators to trace over live-action film to ensure realistic motion. He began his OUT OF THE INK-WELL cartoon series (1916–1929), featuring Koko the Clown, two years later.

Many of the characters in the earliest animated films were taken from newspaper comic strips: "Mutt and Jeff," "the Katzenjammer Kids," "Old Doc Yak." Comics were still relatively new, but enormously popular, and offered a convenient source of familiar, established characters. In fact, Blackton had appeared in a live-action comedy short as Fred Opper's HAPPY HOOLIGAN. Also, many of the early animators had worked as newspaper

BRAY PRODUCTIONS, INC.
PRESENTS

DINKY DOODLE
IN

EGYPT

WRITTEN & DIRECTED
BY
WALTER
LANTZ

Distributed by
FILM BOOKING OFFICES OF AMERICA

cartoonists; even Sidney Smith, the creator of the extremely popular comic strip "The Gumps," briefly tried his hand at animation. Soon a group of characters created specifically for animation appeared, including Bobby Bumps, Dinky Doodle and Bonzo the Dog.

The cartoons were made hastily—as quickly as one a week. Animation was a little stiff and plot and story were virtually nonexistent. Each film was just a series of gags loosely strung together. One animator would simply pick up where another had left off and hope for the best.

In 1919, Felix the Cat, the most popular cartoon character of the next decade, made his debut in FELINE FOLLIES. Created and animated by Otto Messmer at the Pat Sullivan Studio, Felix was the first animated "star" and the first animated character to be the subject of a marketing campaign: toys, games, sheet music, etc. The secret of Felix's popularity lay in the fact that he had something no other studio character had—personality. Messmer developed the techniques McCay had explored in GERTIE to create a character who could be identified by the way he moved. The other cartoon characters of that time moved stiffly around the screen, using formula walks and runs, but not Felix. Messmer, who had studied the films of Charlie Chaplin for an earlier animated series, was able to give Felix a unique walk and a wide range of gestures and expressions.

"I had him sparkling all the time. Most of the cartoon characters (by other studios) were like dummies, just jumping," Messmer explained in an interview with animation historian John Canemaker, "so I used an extreme amount of eye motion, wriggling the eyes and turning the whiskers, and this seemed to be what hit the public—expressions!"

A poster for a "Dinky Doodle" short from the mid-1920's: the cartoon short was an integral part of an afternoon or evening at the movies.

COURTESY OF WALT DISNEY PRODUCTIONS

The Felix walk: the popular cat strikes a characteristic pose on a page from a flip book drawn by Otto Messmer.

COURTESY OF OTTO MESSMER/© FELIX THE CAT PRODUCTIONS, INC. DISTRIBUTED BY KING FEATURES, INC.

Sullivan refused to adapt Felix to sound after 1928, which hurt the popularity of his character. When Sullivan died in 1933, his studio closed, and Felix—already past his prime—passed into animation history. (The character was later revived twice, but without Messmer.) By 1933, the crown had passed to a new animated star, Mickey Mouse.

Walt Disney, the creator of the well-known mouse, began his career as a commercial artist in Kansas City, but had entered the field of animation in the early 1920's with his LAUGH-O-GRAMS and ALICE IN CARTOONLAND series. The latter, a live action/animation combination, gave Disney the impetus to move to Hollywood. There, he introduced his first popular character: Oswald, the Lucky Rabbit. Disney lost the rights to Oswald in 1927 after a dispute with his distributor in

New York. On the return trip to Hollywood, he created the personality of the most famous animated character ever—Mickey Mouse.

While Disney could draw, he could never draw Mickey well. The physical appearance of the character was designed by his associate, the great animator, Ub Iwerks. The character Iwerks created was a rubbery black construction of circles and garden hose limbs, very similar to Oswald, Felix, and a number of other early cartoon characters.

Mickey made his screen debut in 1928, in what was actually his third film: STEAMBOAT WILLIE. (PLANE CRAZY and GALLOPING GAUCHOS, which were intended as silent shorts, were drawn earlier, but released later—with sound tracks.) STEAMBOAT WILLIE was the first synchronized sound cartoon; other animators had experimented with

Ub Iwerks at work, around 1929; he once did more than 500 animation drawings in a single day to win a bet.

STEAMBOAT WILLIE (1927); a loose-limbed Mickey Mouse knocks out "Turkey in the Straw" on pots and pans.

The heroic young tree battles a forest fire in FLOWERS AND TREES (1931).

sound/animation combinations, but it was typical of Disney to perfect the technique before releasing it to the public. STEAMBOAT WILLIE was a sensation, and so was its star—the mouse who could whistle, dance, and play "Turkey in the Straw" on a cow's teeth.

The years between STEAMBOAT WILLIE and the outbreak of World War II were the great era of experimentation in animation at the Disney studio. The artists were given the time and freedom to experiment. Drawing lessons, lectures on a variety of subjects, and screenings of popular films for analysis were provided for the animators. The experiments paid off; vir-tually every technique used by modern ani-mators was discovered or devised there. Disney did little drawing, but he had an unparalleled understanding of story and pacing and insisted that their cartoons be carefully structured.

The tightly plotted and beautifully animated shorts from the Disney studio simply out-classed their rivals. Almost every cartoon from this era represented a breakthrough of some sort. FLOWERS AND TREES (1932) was the first Technicolor cartoon and the first film to win an Oscar in the animated short category.

Three cartoon stars from the Golden Age of studio animation: the inept Elmer Fudd; the affable, "wise guy" rabbit, Bugs Bunny; and the brash, outrageous Daffy Duck.

THE THREE LITTLE PIGS (1933) was a revelation in character animation; it proved that characters who looked alike could demonstrate different personalities if they moved differently. THE OLD MILL (1937) was the first film to use the *multiplane camera* to create an illusion of great depth.

This experimentation was also expensive; many of the early shorts failed to regain their production costs. But the popularity of the characters led to many lines of character merchandise—toys, dolls, soap, games, watches, books—that provided a substantial spin-off income. In fact, the popularity of the

Mickey Mouse handcar toy helped to rescue the Lionel Company from bankruptcy in 1934.

About the same time, many animation studios moved to Hollywood, which had become the center of the motion picture industry. It was in Hollywood that many of the animated "stars" were born. At Warner Brothers, an insane duck named Daffy "woo-hoo-ed" his way through PORKY'S DUCK HUNT in 1937. Three years later, the wildly brilliant Tex Avery brought life to the rabbit who would become Bugs Bunny in A WILD HARE. In 1940,

Walter Lantz (shown here at the Bray Studio in 1924, before he opened his own studio in Hollywood) and his obstreperous wood-pecker, Woody.

SNOW WHITE AND THE SEVEN DWARFS (1937): the first animated fea-ture by an American studio and a milestone in animation history.

William Hanna and Joseph Barbera, then at MGM, scored a big hit with a cat and mouse team called Tom and Jerry.

Walter Lantz introduced what would become his most famous character in the Andy Panda short KNOCK KNOCK: Woody Woodpecker. In that same year, at MGM, two young directors, William Hanna and Joseph Barbera, scored a hit with a cat and mouse team called Tom and Jerry in PUSS GETS THE BOOT. At the Fleischer Studio, a half dog/half girl character made her debut in DIZZY DISHES in 1930; Animator Grim Natwich would transform her into the sexy Betty Boop. Popeye, based on the sailor in Elzie Segar's comic strip, "Thimble Theatre," joined Betty in 1933 in POPEYE THE SAILOR. The Fleischer Studio remained in New York until 1938, when its headquarters were transferred to Miami.

In 1937, Disney scored another first with the release of SNOW WHITE AND THE SEVEN DWARFS. SNOW WHITE was not the first animated feature—there is evidence of one having been done in Argentina as early as 1917, and Lotte Reiniger had released PRINCE ACHMED in 1926—but it was the first studio feature. It was also a beautifully drawn tour de force of character animation. The enormous commercial success of the film saved the studio, as Disney had gambled heavily upon it. Disney followed SNOW WHITE in 1940 with PINOCCHIO, considered by many critics to be the studio's finest feature, and the boldly experimental FANTASIA. Both films were expensive, costing more than $2 million apiece—a considerable sum at the time—but neither was initially a financial success.

Betty Boop, the comic vamp created by Grim Natwich.

Two original cels and backgrounds from the Fleischers' GULLIVER'S TRAVELS (1939): artwork from this studio is extremely rare.

COURTESY OF SCOTT GOLDSTEIN AND NATIONAL TELEFILM ASSOCIATES, INC. EXCLUSIVE WORLDWIDE DISTRIBUTOR OF "GULLIVER'S TRAVELS"

In 1939, the Fleischers released their first feature, GULLIVER'S TRAVELS, loosely based on Jonathan Swift's classic satire, which they followed 2 years later with MR. BUG (HOPPITY) GOES TO TOWN. Neither film was particularly successful, and the timing was bad for both the Fleischers and Disney. The outbreak of World War II destroyed the lucrative overseas market that contributed so much to the success of SNOW WHITE. MR. BUG was released just 3 days before the bombing of Pearl Harbor!

The animated stars of Hollywood devoted themselves to war work as diligently as their live-action counterparts. Animation studios produced military training films, posters to sell bonds, and logos for various units of the armed services. Pluto towed away mines for the insignia of Mine Division 19, U. S. S. Howard, and the logo of Motor Gun Boat #51—London, England, featured Mickey Mouse firing a sling shot from atop a swordfish. Daffy Duck and Donald Duck both tried to evade the draft. The most widely distributed of any of the Warners shorts was Bob Clampett's ANY BONDS TODAY? which featured Bugs Bunny, Porky Pig, and an Army sergeant doing a version of "the Yam." In 1943, Disney and MGM caricatured Hitler in DER FEUHRER'S FACE and THE BLITZ WOLF respectively. At Famous Studios, Superman fought the "Japoteurs" in 1942, while at Warner's, Bugs Bunny marched off to "Tokyo, Berlin, and Points East" singing the Marine's Hymn in his Flatbush accent in SUPER RABBIT (1943). Many animators served in the 18th Air Force Base Unit (First Motion Picture Unit), making training films.

It was also during the 1940's that the Hollywood short cartoon took on definitive form. Disney had established his studio as the

COMET No. 1

© WALT DISNEY

unchallenged master of features and beautiful animation, but MGM and especially Warners excelled in the comic shorts. Fast-paced, brash, violent, and wonderfully funny, the finest short cartoons were made during the 1940's and 1950's by directors like Friz Freleng, Chuck Jones, Bob McKimson, and Bob Clampett at Warners, and Tex Avery, William Hanna, and Joseph Barbera at MGM. When most audiences hear the word "cartoon," they still think of these classic animated comedies, starring Bugs Bunny, Yosemite Sam, Wile E. Coyote, the Roadrunner, Pepe Le Pew, Daffy Duck, Elmer Fudd, Porky Pig, Tom and Jerry, and Droopy.

The Warner Brothers cartoons were among the funniest ever produced in Hollywood. They featured the antics of such popular characters as Bugs Bunny (right), Pepe LePew (left), Wile E. Coyote and the Road Runner, Porky Pig, and Yosemite Sam.

© 1983 WARNER BROTHERS

Friz Freleng's Pink Panther, whose expressions and gestures made words unnecessary. The Panther on the left, drawn with grease pencil, is from one of his first appearances; the Panther on the right represents a more recent version.

© UNITED ARTISTS

Mr. Wile E. Coyote and the Roadrunner.

Porky Pig poses for the camera.

Droopy, Tex Avery's laconic basset hound.

An original cel from HELL-BENT FOR ELECTION (1944), the first film from the UPA Studio, with caricatures of Franklin D. Roosevelt and Thomas E. Dewey as trains.

COURTESY OF NICK AND TEE BOSUSTOW/ © UPA PICTURES, INC.

In 1941, the animation industry was shaken by a strike at the Disney studio. The animators wanted to unionize the studio, a move Disney opposed. The controversy was bitterly fought, and neither side emerged unsullied. Participants on both sides still recall the events with rancour after more than 40 years. A number of artists left Disney to find a studio that would revolutionize the look of animation: UPA.

United Productions of America, or UPA, was formed in 1943 on the proverbial shoestring, with artists working for little or no money whenever they could. The studio began as a partnership between three Disney alumni: Zachary Schwartz, David Hilberman, and Stephen Bosustow (who later bought out the other two). Their first major production was HELL-BENT FOR ELECTION, a campaign film for Franklin Roosevelt, sponsored by the United Auto Workers. Chuck Jones directed the film, working in the evenings, after putting in a full day at Warner's.

Where Disney animation had always stressed three-dimensionality and realism, the artists at UPA preferred a flat, stylized look, taken from contemporary graphics. Instead of the gentle tales Disney favored, they sought to inject social and political comment into their work with films like THE BROTHERHOOD OF MAN and THE HANGMAN. Because their financial resources were small, they could not afford the lavish style of Disney and had to work in *limited animation*. Limited animation used fewer drawings and placed an emphasis on key poses; strong stories and sound tracks helped to carry the animation.

UPA changed the look of animation with award-winning films like THE UNICORN IN THE GARDEN, THE TELL-TALE HEART, ROOTY-TOOT-TOOT, and MADELINE. Later, the studio produced the popular characters of Mr. Magoo (1949) and Gerald McBoing Boing (1951). The bright, clean look of the UPA films caught on—Disney even began to use it in films like TOOT, WHISTLE, PLUNK AND BOOM (1953).

The 1950's also saw the demise of the Hollywood short. These cartoons were fairly expensive to produce; by the end of the decade, a Bugs Bunny short cost about $35,000 (approximately one-fourth of what it would cost today). No short film could earn that much in theatre rentals. The animation departments of the various studios had been kept alive by the practice of "block booking": If a theatre owner wanted to show a studio's big feature, the owner also had to take a second feature, a cartoon, and sometimes a newsreel, as a package deal. But the Supreme Court struck down the practice in 1948. It became increasingly apparent in the mid-1950's that the cartoons were costing more to produce than theatre owners were willing to pay to show them, and the animation units of the studios were disbanded.

But there was another potential market for animation: the new medium of television. Many studios sold the rights to broadcast their old cartoons for lump sums. These cartoons are still being rerun with respectable ratings after three decades. The problem with doing animation for television was that so much material was required in so short a time that it seemed impossible to produce it fast enough. Jay Ward began experimenting with CRUSADER RABBIT in 1949, which used very limited animation and clever scripts.

ROOTY-TOOT-TOOT (1952): the daintily murderous Frankie embraces the lawyer who got her acquitted of shooting Johnny, who done her wrong.

COURTESY OF NICK AND TEE BOSUSTOW/ © UPA PICTURES, INC.

Gerald McBoing Boing: the popular UPA character, taken from a story by Dr. Seuss, starred in a series of theatrical shorts and a television program.

COURTESY OF NICK AND TEE BOSUSTOW/ © UPA PICTURES, INC.

Yogi Bear, one of Hanna-Barbera's most popular characters, with his sidekick, Booboo. During the late 1970's, Yogi and Booboo were revived for Saturday morning television.

Ruff (the bulldog) and Reddy (the cat), the title characters from Hanna-Barbera's first animated-for-television program. "They sometimes have their little spats/Even fight like dogs and cats/But when they need each other/That's when they're rough and ready!"

But it was the Oscar-winning directors of MGM's TOM AND JERRY series, William Hanna and Joseph Barbera, who discovered the way to make television animation pay. In 1957, they premiered their first animated-for-television show from their newly founded studio: RUFF AND REDDY, a comedy/adventure about a dog and a cat. The animation was even more limited than the cartoons from UPA, but it was colorful and clean-looking, and proved to be quite popular. RUFF AND REDDY was followed by a number of popular animated shows: HUCKLEBERRY HOUND, YOGI BEAR, QUICK DRAW MCGRAW, THE FLINTSTONES, et al.

The 1960's were dark days for animation in America, as the art form came to be identified with Saturday morning TV shows and children's programming. Animation became increasingly limited as costs rose and network schedules required more and more hours of film—trends which continue to this day. Animation grew more and more popular in Japan, with television programs and features being produced for domestic consumption. In America and Europe, independent filmmakers, commercial animators, and smaller studios, especially Zagreb in Yugoslavia and the National Film Board of Canada, began to fill the aesthetic void left by the demise of the Hollywood studios.

Many animation studios had been founded in Eastern Europe after World War II; animators seemed to enjoy greater freedom of expression than their live-action counterparts under the Soviet-dominated governments. Relatively little has been written about their films or about the animation produced in the Soviet Union. The best known of these Eastern European studios is Zagreb in Yugoslavia. The Zagreb Studio was founded in the mid-1950's by a group of artists and animators who had been inspired by the films of UPA; these artists continued to experiment with limited animation, interesting stories, and provocative graphics. For example, ERSATZ, which won the Oscar in 1961, drew heavily on the style of the painter Vasily Kandinsky. Many of the Zagreb films were charming and even striking, and the studio remained an important artistic influence on world animation throughout the 1960's.

The animation unit of the National Film Board of Canada was established in 1942, under the innovative filmmaker Norman McLaren. Although its stated goal (like the rest of the Film Board's units) was "to interpret Canada to Canadians and people of other lands," by the 1960's the Board had become an international center of creative animation. By the end of the decade, it had supplanted Zagreb as *the* home of individual creativity in animation—a position it has maintained to the present. A measure of the quality of the work done at the Film Board can be seen in the fact that between 1970 and 1980, seven of their films were nominated for Oscars, and three won: SAND CASTLE in 1977, SPECIAL DELIVERY in 1978, and EVERY CHILD in 1979. Films from the Board are regularly shown at festivals and contests around the world.

As the 1960's came to a close, American animation arose like a phoenix from its ashes. The craze for nostalgia led to a rediscovery of animation from the "golden age" of the 1930's, 1940's, and early 1950's. People once again delighted in the "ricky-ticky" animation of the Betty Boop shorts and the still-fresh humor of the Warner cartoons. Children who had grown up watching the limited animation of Saturday morning television discovered the beauty and power of full animation.

Another important factor in the rebirth of interest in animation was the popularity of two films: YELLOW SUBMARINE (1967) and FRITZ THE CAT (1972). YELLOW SUBMARINE, directed by Canadian animator, George Dunning, was one of the great "head trip" films of the late 1960's; ironically, one of its greatest rivals was FANTASIA. The use of contemporary graphics

The highly stylized graphics of Heinz Edelman gave a bold look to George Dunning's YELLOW SUBMARINE (1967).

Animation director Ralph Bakshi with four characters from his feature, AMERICAN POP: Zalmie, Benny, Tony, and Little Pete.

was not new, but the bold, colorful style of artists like Peter Max was; and the enormous popularity of the Beatles' music gave the film a ready-made audience. While the story of this brightly colored fantasy seems rather weak today, some sequences of YELLOW SUBMARINE remain visually brilliant.

By the end of the 1960's, a large audience was ready and eager for an X-rated animated feature; a young animator from New York named Ralph Bakshi provided it. Based on the adventures of Robert Crumb's underground "comix" character, FRITZ THE CAT was a great commercial success and something of an artistic revelation. American audiences had never seen animation used to present such harsh, gritty subject matter before. Bakshi has continued to make animated features that have been the subject of controversy, both for their content and their style, including HEAVY TRAFFIC, WIZARDS, THE LORD OF THE RINGS, and AMERICAN POP.

At the beginning of the 1970's, American animation faced a major crisis. For decades, studios had been depending on older, usually Disney-trained animators to draw their films. As these men began to retire, filmmakers became painfully aware of the dearth of well-trained young animators. Belatedly, studios began training and recruiting programs all over the world, searching for talented young artists. Animation classes became increasingly popular in colleges and art schools, with

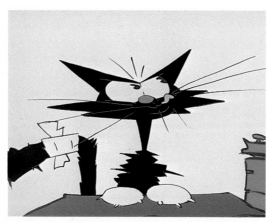

young animators creating interesting and imaginative films. The talent search continues, but a weird dichotomy persists in the animation industry—almost all the artists are either over 55 or under 35. Network programming continued to be dominated by Saturday morning animation, most of it produced by Hanna-Barbera (SCOOBY-DOO, CAPTAIN CAVEMAN, GODZILLA, and JOSÉ AND THE PUSSYCATS), Filmation (FAT ALBERT, STAR TREK, and THE ARCHIES), and De Patie–Freleng (THE PINK PANTHER).

And while the studios were sorting out where the future animators would be coming from, animation took a new turn, towards special effects, riding on the popularity of science fiction and fantasy films, from 2001: A SPACE ODYSSEY to STAR WARS and THE EMPIRE STRIKES BACK. The glittering futuristic look of STAR WARS also gave impetus to the growing use of computer animation in films, commercials, and network logos.

With the costs of live-action filmmaking rising so high that animation has become competitive, especially in the area of television commercials; with numerous features and television specials in production around the world; with new studios being established, specializing in every area of animation from commercials to features; with computer and conventional animation equipment growing more sophisticated; with audience attendance at animated features and festivals steadily increasing; the future of animation at the beginning of the 1980's looks brighter than it has since the early 1930's. A new "golden age" may be at hand.

Oscar Grillo's SEASIDE WOMAN, a joyous updating of the stylized graphics of the 1920's.

Technicians manipulate a model of an Imperial Walker for a stop-motion sequence in THE EMPIRE STRIKES BACK.

State-of-the-art animation: a three dimensional computer-generated flight simulation over a landscape for Network Nine, Australia.

Glittering shapes and colors for a commercial for Schneider Television, West Germany.

2

Animation Techniques

The general term "animation" covers a variety of filmmaking techniques, all of which have one of two characteristics: they require the filmmaker to work frame by frame or they *create* motion instead of record it. Live-action film is made in takes and scenes that may last a few seconds or several minutes; animation requires the artist to adjust the image—whether by changing a drawing under the camera or slightly altering the position of a puppet's limbs—for every frame of film, or 24 adjustments for every second of screen time. Live-action film *records* motions: Every movement, from the flicker of Groucho Marx's eyebrows to the swing of Errol Flynn's sabre, was performed and captured on film. But until the animators' drawings were photographed, Mickey Mouse never waved "hello" and Bugs Bunny never crunched a carrot. All animated actions are illusions of motion because the movements do not and cannot exist except on film.

This chapter explores the principal techniques of animation, the materials and methods used to produce the films that have delighted, intrigued, and educated audiences since the invention of the art form at the beginning of this century.

TWO-DIMENSIONAL TECHNIQUES
1. Cel Animation
Cel animation is the classic method used to create most familiar cartoons, from the Disney features to the Hollywood shorts to Saturday morning television programs. The name derives from the sheets of clear acetate called "cels" (because they were originally made of celluloid) onto which the animators' drawings are traced. Since its invention in 1915, the cel technique has been the standard in the animation industry. The process is described in detail in Chapter 3.

2. Drawn on Paper
Cel animation, which produces a hard-edged image with flat areas of color encased in outlines, is not suited to the look of every film or to every artist's drawing style. Some animators prefer to work in traditional drawing media to create a softer, more shaded quality that preserves the textures of their original drawings and of the paper.

For her award-winning film FURIES, Sara Petty drew in charcoal on rough paper and colored each drawing with oil pastels. More than 2,000 finished drawings were required for a film not quite 3 minutes long that depicted the movements of her pet cats. The result was a delicately shimmering world of colors which subtly shifted as the forms of the cats underwent metamorphoses.

Animation on paper by Ryan Larkin: (top) the god Pan and the nymph Syrinx rendered in charcoal for SYRINX; (bottom) An ink wash figure from WALKING, which Larkin described as an expression of "the pure delight of movement."

COURTESY OF THE NATIONAL FILM BOARD OF CANADA

To evoke the desire of the god Pan in his film SYRINX (1965), Ryan Larkin used a few charcoal drawings, which he altered every few frames under the camera by erasing or adding lines and shading. This technique produced a sensual, atmospheric look, well-suited to the Debussy music he was illustrating. For WALKING (1966) and STREET MUSIQUE (1972), the same artist used ink washes on paper, taking advantage of the spontaneous patterns formed by the different colors and thicknesses of the inks as they dried, and of the subtle puckerings the wet ink produced in the paper.

The Oscar winner for an animated short in 1978, SPECIAL DELIVERY, was drawn in colored pencil. The constantly shifting colors matched the style of the animation, which shifted in perspective. Eunice Macauley, who co-directed the film, explained succinctly why the drawings for the film were so much smaller than standard animation drawings (only about 5″ x 6½″ as opposed to 10½″ x 12½″): "They don't take as long to fill in."

Like most drawn-on-paper films, these examples are short, personal statements by individual artists. The amount of work required to do so many finished drawings makes this type of animation impractical for a feature.

3. Cutouts

Cutout animation uses small jointed figures that are placed under the animation camera and carefully manipulated to create the illusion of movement. Usually, the figures are made of heavy paper or light cardboard that is thin enough to be cut easily into small shapes, but strong enough to survive repeated handling. The joints for the limbs can be made in varied ways: with small interlocking loops of string; tiny pins or wires; or brass paper fasteners, with their tops concealed under circles of colored paper. The figures

may be finely finished with carefully drawn details, or they may be just simple shapes of paper. Different sizes of each character can be used to give the illusion of close-ups and long shots, and multiple heads can be used for changes of expression.

The great artist of cutout animation was Lotte Reiniger (see Chapter 6), who created intricate worlds out of cut paper, including THE ADVENTURES OF PRINCE ACHMED. Recently, artists have begun to use cutouts in semiabstract films, very different from Reiniger's silhouette depictions of fairy tales. In TANGRAM, Alan Slasor took a series of simple geometric shapes, based on an early Chinese system of design, and combined them to make stylized animals.

Cutout animation is also popular with beginners and school children because relatively little preparation is needed before the actual process of animation begins. Once the figures have been completed, they are laid on top of the backgrounds under the camera and lights. The figures are moved slightly before each picture is taken. A brief cutout film can be made in just a few days.

4. Cutouts on Cels

Some animators prefer to combine cutouts and cels to take advantage of the opportunities offered by each technique. The animator does the drawings on paper, then cuts out the figures and pastes them onto cels. This allows the animator to use shading and pencil techniques on the characters, but frees him or her from having to redraw the background for every frame. A recent example of cutouts on cels is Bretislav Pojar's film E. Placing these drawings on cels allowed him to use fairly detailed backgrounds done in the same media. To have done the film entirely on paper would have required many hundreds of hours of tedious redrawing.

5. Photokinesis

This is a highly specialized technique that involves moving a static piece of artwork under the camera to produce an illusion of movement on the screen. Usually, the artwork is something that would be difficult or impossible to animate by conventional techniques: photographs, pictures from magazines, collages, reproductions of paintings. The artwork is usually combined with similar types of images cut out and pasted onto cels. Because the viewer is not used to seeing these things move, the effect is often striking.

Frank Mouris used literally thousands of images cut from magazines and catalogs to

make FRANK FILM, a vast, complicated collage that is both an autobiography and a satire of society's consumerism. It won the Oscar in 1973 (see Chapter 6). Mike Jittlov combined material from magazines, catalogs, and pattern envelopes for ANIMATO, a film designed as a show reel for department stores to demonstrate the kind of commercials he could make for them.

Another variation of the photokinesis technique has been used very effectively by Dan McLaughlin and Chuck Braverman. Hundreds of still images are shot for two or three frames apiece, so they appear on the screen for just a fraction of a second. This rapid juxtaposition of images produces an overview of a subject—

GOD IS DOG SPELLED BACKWARDS, Dan McLaughlin's survey of Western Art: each image is held for two frames—one-twelfth of a second on the screen

© DAN MCLAUGHLIN

the history of western art or of a decade—that goes by so quickly the pictures register almost subliminally. Enormous amounts of information can be communicated this way.

Although photokinesis sounds relatively simple, it is surprisingly difficult to do well; it requires an exceptional sense of design, an eye for the powerful image, and an absolute mastery of camera technique to produce an effective film.

THREE-DIMENSIONAL TECHNIQUES

Three-dimensional or stop-motion animation has certain affinities with live-action filmmaking. Sets—which may range from simple backdrops to elaborate miniatures—must be constructed and lighted. A motion picture camera with a single-frame capability is used. But like two-dimensional animation, stop-motion filmmaking is used to *create* motions, rather than record them. The filmmaker must possess the same understanding of how and why things and people move as they do to create a convincing film. The object is photographed for one frame, moved slightly, photographed again, moved slightly, photographed again, etc. Several hours may be required to shoot a few seconds of stop-motion animation.

1. Puppet Animation

The term "puppet animation" is generally used to describe the frame-by-frame filming of three-dimensional figures with articulated joints. The puppet may be made out of a variety of materials: sponge rubber, wood, cloth, and plastic are commonly used. Almost all puppets have an armature, a jointed metal skeleton that supports the figure. An armature is a delicate apparatus, and great skill is required to create one. Steel rods act like the long bones of a human or animal skeleton. The joints—tiny hinges or ball-and-socket assemblies—must be flexible enough to move

in increments of a fraction of an inch, but stable enough to hold a position once it has been set. Wires are often used to articulate fingers, toes, claws, and other small joints. The body material is attached to the armature or, in the case of plastic foam, molded onto it. The surface may be textured or covered with animal hide to suggest skin, fur, or whatever the puppet requires. The finished puppet is usually a recognizable character or animal.

Sometimes a puppet resembles a marionette or a hand puppet. Films of this type are especially popular in areas of the world where there is a strong tradition of puppet theatre, such as Eastern Europe. One of the greatest artists of the puppet film was the Czech animator Jiri Trnka. Among his best known works are a handsome adaptation of Shakespeare's A MIDSUMMER NIGHT'S DREAM and THE HAND, a moving parable of tyranny.

Co Hoedman won the Oscar in 1977 for a very different sort of puppet film, SAND CASTLE. In this gentle fantasy, strange creatures made of sponge rubber build a world for themselves out of a sand dune, only to be buried by the wind-blown sand.

(Far left) A collage of images cut from magazines by Frank Mouris.

© 1981 FRANK MOURIS

SAND CASTLE by Co Hoedman: the creator, a figure of carved sponge rubber, begins to fashion one of his assistants in this gentle fantasy.

COURTESY OF THE NATIONAL FILM BOARD OF CANADA

Puppet animation techniques have also been used to create monsters and special effects in many live-action science fiction films. The puppet-monsters are photographed on miniature sets, and the resulting film is combined with the live-action footage of actors by various techniques. One of the greatest practitioners of this type of stop-motion animation is Ray Harryhausen, who created such memorable creatures as the giant ape in MIGHTY JOE YOUNG, the title monster in THE BEAST FROM 20,000 FATHOMS, and the skeletons that fight the hero of JASON AND THE ARGONAUTS. (The latter sequence took 4½ months to film.) More recently, stop-motion techniques have been used to create such effects as the Imperial Walkers and Luke Skywalker's Tauntaun in THE EMPIRE STRIKES BACK. Obviously, exceptional skill is needed to sculpt and manipulate such intricate and realistic puppets.

2. Object Animation

The key difference between puppet and object animation is that, in the latter, the object retains its identity. The viewer is always aware that he is looking at a moving bean or lump of clay; the object is not perceived as a character, as is usually the case with puppet animation. The basic technique of moving something very slightly before each frame is photographed is essentially the same.

Object animation is occasionally done in two dimensions on a regular animation stand. Using Chinese brushes, Ishu Patel manipulated thousands of tiny, brightly colored glass beads to tell a parable of evolution in BEAD GAME. Other two-dimensional object films have used such unlikely materials as bits of cork, fragments of linoleum, and cookies.

Three-dimensional object animation involves camera, set, and lighting arrangements similar to those used in puppet animation. Almost anything can be animated by an artist with sufficient talent, imagination, and patience. John Brister used groups of tangerines to spoof the Busby Berkely routines of 1930's musicals in MANDARIN ORANGES. For a John Denver television special, John Wukaluk

Phil Tippet animates a model of Luke Skywalker's Tauntaun for THE EMPIRE STRIKES BACK.

A world of children's blocks: stop-motion animation by Co Hoedman for TCHOU TCHOU.

made melons dance to "Thank God I'm a Country Boy," while a pumpkin with stringy hair, a floppy hat, and little round glasses did the song in lip sync. Co Hoedman created a world of children's blocks for his charming film TCHOU TCHOU.

Object animation is also a popular method for teaching filmmaking to schoolchildren. They learn the elements of animation by maneuvering their favorite dolls and toys in front of the camera.

3. Clay Animation

For many years, clay animation was seen as a minor variant of object animation. The pliable texture of clay lent itself to the tiny manipulations needed for stop-motion animation but it tended to melt or dry out under the hot lights. Clay was a popular medium for children's films because it was cheap, easy to use, and readily available. A few serious animators like Oskar Fischinger experimented with clay animation, and Art Clokey did his popular GUMBY series using clay. But clay was generally perceived as a crude medium, unsuited to fine animation.

In 1974, Will Vinton and Bob Gardiner proved otherwise. In their Oscar-winning film CLOSED MONDAYS, they demonstrated a revolutionary technique that could produce subtle, lifelike nuances of expression and complicated movements and metamorphoses. They called it "Claymation."® Each Claymation figure was built around an armature similar to those used in puppet animation. The metal skeleton was covered with layers of subtly colored clay that were sculpted to suggest flesh and clothing. The story of CLOSED MONDAYS involves a drunken man who stumbles into a closed art museum and sees the various paintings come to life. The high point of this short occurs when he switches on a kinetic sculpture that transforms itself into a robot, a globe, a fist with a hand at the end of each finger, and a bust of Albert Einstein.

Vinton and Gardiner subsequently dissolved their partnership, but each has continued to produce sophisticated clay animation films. Gardiner, who is best known for the ecological public service spots he has done for television, works on various film and writing projects. Vinton maintains a studio in Portland, Oregon, and has produced a number of award-winning films, including THE LEGEND OF RIP VAN WINKLE, THE LITTLE PRINCE, and the trailers for Bette Midler's concert film DIVINE MADNESS.

The work of these two men has done much to win recognition for clay animation as a valid medium for artistic expression and has inspired many students and independent filmmakers to work with clay.

CLOSED MONDAYS: the astonishingly realistic expressions and movements in this film demonstrated the real potential of clay animation.

The title character from Will Vinton's THE LITTLE PRINCE.

A clay bust of Bette Midler joins the presidents on Mt. Rushmore in the trailer for the film DIVINE MADNESS.

Will Vinton's Oscar-nominated short CREATION: streaks of colored clay on plexiglass create the effect of an oil painting in motion.

4. Pixilation

Pixilation is the animation technique closest to live-action filmmaking. Props and live actors are photographed frame-by-frame to create an illusion of motion—usually zany, impossible, speeded-up motion. In his popular film THE WIZARD OF SPEED AND TIME, Mike Jittlov, as the green-robed wizard, seems to zoom through Hollywood at 500 mph. He later leads an array of cameras, tripods, and lights through a precision dance routine.

In 1952, the brilliant filmmaker Norman McLaren proved that pixilation could be used for serious films with his Oscar-winning short NEIGHBORS. In this parable about violence and aggression, two men live at peace, side by side, until a single flower springs up at the boundary between their yards. The battle for possession of it escalates until the houses, the men, and the flower have been destroyed. "If all my films were to be destroyed except one," said McLaren in a rare, recent interview, "I would want that one to be NEIGHBORS because I feel it has a permanent message about human nature."

5. Computer Animation

Computer animation represents a convergence of trends from the widely disparate fields of computer science, abstract art, and animation. The capabilities of computers to generate visual displays of their problem-solving activities were first used in relatively simple matters: vector graphics or simulating a grid structure to test a design for stress resistance. As the equipment grew more sophisticated, so did the work. Computer simulations have been used to demonstrate the three-dimensional structure of organic molecules, helping researchers to understand them and to design drugs; to illustrate how various factors can affect the growth of a sea shell; to simulate conditions for training astronauts, pilots, and sea captains; to reveal how an object would be affected in a wind tunnel. Computer animation is still used in many areas of research today, although this work receives little publicity.

While artists had begun to explore the possibilities of abstract filmmaking as long ago as the early 1920's, one of the major problems they faced was difficulty in making the many drawings required to move a complicated abstract pattern for even a few seconds. The number of drawings needed meant that most abstract films were very short. Only a few artists were willing—or able—to dedicate the large amounts of time required to make even a brief film.

The essential figure bridging the gap between computer science and nonobjective films was John Whitney. For years, Whitney and his brother, James, had been experimenting with abstract films. The increasingly sophisticated equipment John built out of war surplus materials, and the complex results he sought to obtain from it, gradually led him to employ computer technology.

A single flower springs up between suburban yards and precipitates a war in Norman McLaren's Oscar-winning parable of human aggression, NEIGHBORS.

It would take an animator many years to draw the thousands of colored dots that form the elaborate patterns in Whitney's beautiful film ARABESQUE, but a correctly programmed computer can generate each pattern in a sequence quickly and effortlessly. The pattern is produced on a high-resolution video screen; this image is filmed and color is added later in an optical printer.

Whitney has sought to create an abstract graphic language, comparable to that which exists for music. But many techniques developed from his work are being used to create special effects in science fiction films. Among these techniques is the slit-screen scanning process used to produce the dazzling trip through hyperspace in 2001: A SPACE ODYSSEY.

The space program contributed to the growing sophistication of computer visualizations with the detailed simulations needed for training astronauts and fine-tuning equipment. From the space industry also came the technology that enables a computer to move a piece of equipment precisely through a pattern an infinite number of times. Computer-controlled camera techniques are often combined with stop-motion animation to produce highly effective results, like the extremely lifelike dragon in the recent film DRAGONSLAYER. This technology has been adapted for theatrical lighting and to create flashy light shows in urban discos.

The popularity of science-fiction films such as STAR WARS has, in turn, given rise to an entire school of animated commercials and logos, characterized by glittering chrome letters and zooms into infinite perspective. (Some filmmakers have begun to imitate this high-tech

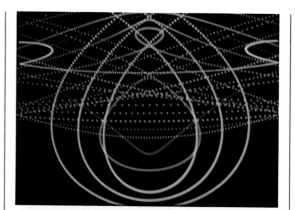

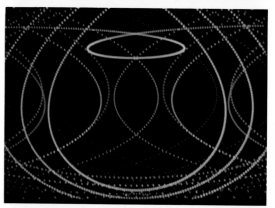

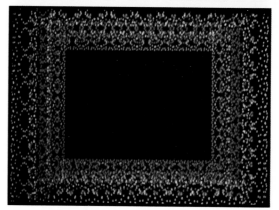

49

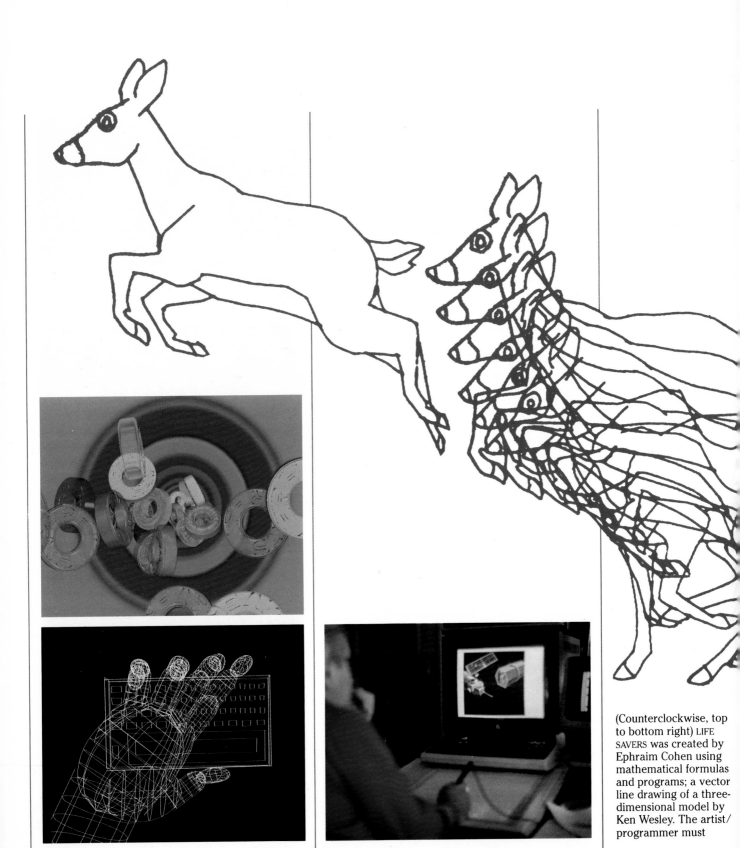

(Counterclockwise, top to bottom right) LIFE SAVERS was created by Ephraim Cohen using mathematical formulas and programs; a vector line drawing of a three-dimensional model by Ken Wesley. The artist/ programmer must

A deer sequence of computer animation generated using the 'tween' system: Extreme frames of the deer's motion (upper left, lower right) were traced into the system using an electric pen. The center art is a composite frame of in-between interpolations generated by the 'tween' program. Conventionally, these "in-betweens" would be drawn by an artist. After the line drawings are generated, they are printed and composited with the backgrounds and recorded on tape one frame at a time.

(Right) ANT FARM by Dick Lundin.

look with conventional animation techniques or combinations of computer and cel animation.) The basis of this imagery is the ability of the computer to assign a color (a combination of red, blue, and green) and a value for brightness to each point on a video screen. Increasingly sophisticated programs enable artists to produce three-dimensional objects.

enter all the data to describe a three-dimensional image. Once done, the image can be rotated and manipulated from any point of view; artist Paul Xander at a computer workstation.

Because computers can maintain perfect perspective over an infinite distance, generate flashes and sparkles from a given light source, or change the camera's point of view to any angle, these flashy logos are relatively easy to create. Artists and technicians specializing in computer graphics are more interested in other areas of experimentation. The cutting edge of computer animation techniques involves moving three-dimensional shaded objects in space, rendering textures accurately, and creating a feeling of naturalism and realistic movement—very different from the high-tech flash.

Whether or not computers will ever be used for character animation is the subject of widespread debate. There have been some experiments in that area, but the results have not been particularly successful. Some artists feel that because computers have no emotions, they are incapable of understanding the feelings and stresses that produce the nuances of movement needed to bring an animated character to life. Some computer experts respond that it is simply a question of improving the equipment and/or programs and the interaction between the computer and the human artist, that it is only a matter of time before the computer joins the list of standard animation tools.

The widespread use of personal computers by small business and private individuals has produced a growing demand for graphics capabilities, including animation programs. The potential offered by this software is staggering: programs already exist that can generate over 16 million distinct colors—more than twice as many as the human eye can discern.

Computer flash: Glittering letters and the rings of Saturn were created for the rock group Styx.

COURTESY OF MIDOCEAN GRAPHICS PRODUCTIONS

A car drives through a city of light in a commercial for a radio station.

COURTESY OF MARKS & MARKS/JAM PRODUCTIONS

Two animation techniques created by Caroline Leaf: (top) sand on glass for THE OWL WHO MARRIED A GOOSE and (bottom) paint on glass for THE STREET, based on a story by Mordecai Richler.

While professional animators, film studio employees, and computer scientists will continue to explore the most advanced techniques, the proliferation of computer technology is making it increasingly possible for any individual to create computer animation in the office or at home.

6. Other Techniques

Individual artists continue to devise and develop new animation techniques that reflect their special interests and talents. Some of these new techniques require sophisticated equipment and specialized skills; others are surprisingly simple.

Caroline Leaf, an artist at the National Film Board of Canada, uses sand to make films. "It's beach sand," she explains, "fine, white, and smooth. All I need for one film is as much as will fit in a yogurt container! And I can go on using it for 6 months." She places the sand on a sheet of underlit Plexiglas material under the camera, and sculpts flat figures out of it, using paint brushes. The different thicknesses of the sand create patterns of darker and lighter grays. She manipulates the figures with brushes to create vivid characters and fluid movements in films like THE OWL WHO MARRIED A GOOSE.

Using a similar technique, she maneuvered colored inks and paints on glass to evoke the urban, Jewish milieu of Mordecai Richler's short story THE STREET. One of the drawbacks of these techniques is that no artwork exists after shooting a sequence. In case of a mistake or problem with the camera, the artist would have to start over from scratch, unlike cels and drawings which can always be rephotographed.

Abstract characters from Norman McLaren's drawn-on-film short BLINKETY BLANK.

Many filmmakers have experimented with drawing, painting, or scratching images directly onto 35 mm film stock. Len Lye made COLOUR BOX, the first painted-on-film animation, in 1935. These techniques readily lend themselves to the creation of moving abstractions of color, line, and form. However, in films like HEN HOP, BLINKETY BLANK, and V FOR VICTORY, Norman McLaren demonstrated that recognizable linear figures could be animated this way. Patience, skill with a fine pen, brush, or stylus, and careful attention to matching the image in each frame are required to produce drawn-on-film animation.

A striking technique for animation was invented in the early 1930's by the late husband-and-wife team Alexander Alexeieff and Claire Parker. Alexeieff was a book illustrator who wanted to create films that would capture the textured gray shadings of his etchings. To achieve this effect, Alexeieff and his wife invented the pin screen, a device that uses the shadows of one million tiny headless pins to produce shimmering gray pointillist images, reminiscent of charcoal drawings. The first film created with this technique was an eerie atmospheric version of Mussorgsky's NIGHT ON BALD MOUNTAIN done in 1933.

A scene from Jacques Drouin's pinscreen film MINDSCAPE.

The late Alexander Alexeieff and Claire Parker working on the pinscreen.

Very few pin screen films have been made. The process is quite difficult, and only Alexeieff and Parker, and a few of their students, like Jacques Drouin, have really mastered it. Drouin's LE PAYSAGISTE (MINDSCAPE) has become a staple of animation festivals around the world. An artist paints a landscape and walks into his picture, exploring the surreal fantasy world he finds within it. The somber but luminous imagery of the film has a haunting quality not easily forgotten.

As long as individual artists with special talents and tastes continue to work in animation, new techniques will be invented. The only restraints are the artists' imaginations and their abilities to realize their visions.

Like snowflakes and fingerprints, no two animation studios are exactly alike. At a large studio that produces theatrical features, there may be several directors and designers at work on a single film; at a small commercial house, the director may also be the designer and one of the key animators.

A studio may have its own "in-house" ink-and-paint and camera departments, or private contractors may be hired to do this work as needed. Each animator may have an office or a desk at the studio, or the artists may work in their homes and bring in the finished drawings once a week. The size of the studio, its resources, the types of films it produces, and the talents and interests of the artists involved will determine its structure. But all animated films have the same basic requirements, and this chapter will describe how animation is done at a "typical" studio.

At any individual studio, some of the jobs described in this section may be combined or subdivided; there are no rules that must be followed. But however different the structures of various studios may be, their films all share one feature: Every one begins as an idea, an idea that must be communicated to an audience, an idea that requires the special potential of the animation medium to achieve its maximum effect. Each individual contributes to this idea through his or her talents, helping to clarify and develop it, so that the film the audience sees is the best possible realization of the original idea that can be made.

1. The Writer

Writing for animation is both similar and dissimilar to writing for live-action. Scripts for both kinds of film look superficially alike: Columns of print fill each page, giving the dialogue and descriptions of the action. But animation writers have a different vocabulary of effects and techniques to use than their live-action counterparts. Facial close-ups or shots of the expression in an actress's eyes can be highly effective in live-action but are of little use in animation. Conversely, the animation writer is not limited by minor concerns such as gravity, and can send characters to the moon as easily as to the corner supermarket. Elaborate explosions, opulent settings, and fire-breathing monsters that would be impossible or prohibitively expensive to use in a live-action film can be done relatively easily in an animated one.

The first question that should be asked about any animation script is why should the film be done in animation. A story that involves nothing but realistic human characters in everyday situations will probably be easier to do in live-action, and the results more effective. Animation is a medium of caricature, based on exaggerated depictions of actions

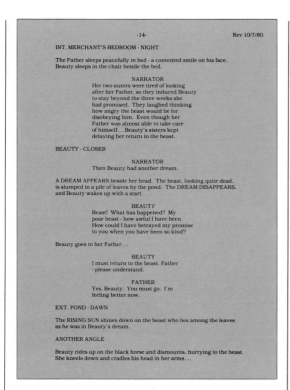

A page from the script of BEAUTY AND THE BEAST, from the "Misunderstood Monsters Series," a CBS Library Special by Bosustow Entertainment.

and expressions. When it is used to present real life too literally, the results are almost always uninteresting. Probably the least successful sequence in Disney's SLEEPING BEAUTY is the scene where Aurora and Prince Philip dance in the forest. It is beautifully animated, but the characters are far less interesting than the more broadly drawn Malificent.

Animation can bring life to dinosaurs that have been dead for 100 million years or to dragons that have never really lived at all. It can turn a gray rabbit into a vivid, wise-cracking personality or make an elephant fly. A good script for an animated film will show an awareness of this potential in the characters and situations it describes.

But a good animation script must contain more than visual fireworks. Not even the most beautiful animation can cover up a weak story or make up for unconvincing characters. A good story for animation is always a good story first, and the writer must understand plot, pacing, structure, and characterization—essential elements of any story. One of the key factors in the success of the great Disney features like PINOCCHIO is their carefully refined structure and pacing.

2. The Producer

The role of the producer varies widely in animation. The producer may be an investor who finances the film, or an animation director with an interest in administration who fills both jobs for a television special. Usually, the producer is the chief administrator of the film. The job includes overseeing the budget and trying to keep the production costs within limits, hiring and firing the staff for the film, and ensuring that it is completed on schedule. The producer may also handle such legal and financial transactions as negotiating the contracts for the voice artists, securing the rights to the story on which the film is based, dealing with distributors, and arranging for the foreign release of the film or its sale to commercial outlets or cable television.

Producer Lorraine Roberts has a wide range of responsibilities at Kurtz and Friends.

COURTESY OF KURTZ AND FRIENDS

Producer-director Chuck Jones at his drawing table: his work ranges from theatrical shorts and features to television specials.

3. The Director

The director of an animated film is the artistic head of the project. It is the director who approves the final designs and the animation, interprets the script and communicates his or her vision of it to the other people involved in the production, and oversees the day-to-day work of the studio.

Many animation directors have personal styles as distinct and recognizable as those of the best live-action directors. Anyone who sees many of the Warner Brothers cartoons learns to distinguish among the wild exaggerations of Tex Avery, the highly verbal humor of Friz Freleng, the delicately balanced combination of verbal and physical gags of Chuck Jones, and the anarchic insanity of Bob Clampett. Yet all four men worked for the same studio and used many of the same characters.

The director (who almost invariably began his or her career as an animator or an assistant) does key drawings for each scene or sequence, indicating the poses of the characters, their most extreme expressions, and how the action fits within the setting and the frame.

The director must understand the characters thoroughly and be able to explain their personalities in words and drawings so that the animators will be able to make them move like the unique individuals they should be.

The director must also understand the medium of animation and be able to use its techniques effectively. The abilities to time a gag, build suspense within a scene, and use images to elicit the reaction wanted from the audience are needed. The director must also know when to cut a scene and where to use a close-up or a long shot. Pacing and timing are especially important in an animated film because the characters cannot hold the audience's attention by themselves, as good live-action actors can.

Unlike the live-action director, the animation director's work is all done before any film is shot. A live-action director can shoot several takes of each scene and cut the best parts together during the editing process; live-action directors usually shoot at least ten times as much film as they finally use. An animation director does not have this luxury: It's important to know what every frame of the film will look like in advance. Because it is so carefully planned and because animation is so difficult to do, very little postproduction editing is done. Three-time Oscar winner Chuck Jones comments: "I don't know of any live-action director who can bear the thought of working the way we do—backwards. All the editing is done in advance. After-the-fact editing on the Warners' shorts probably averaged about 1 percent of the total film—it was never more than 3 to 4 percent, and that was only when the picture ran long." (They had to average 6 minutes apiece.)

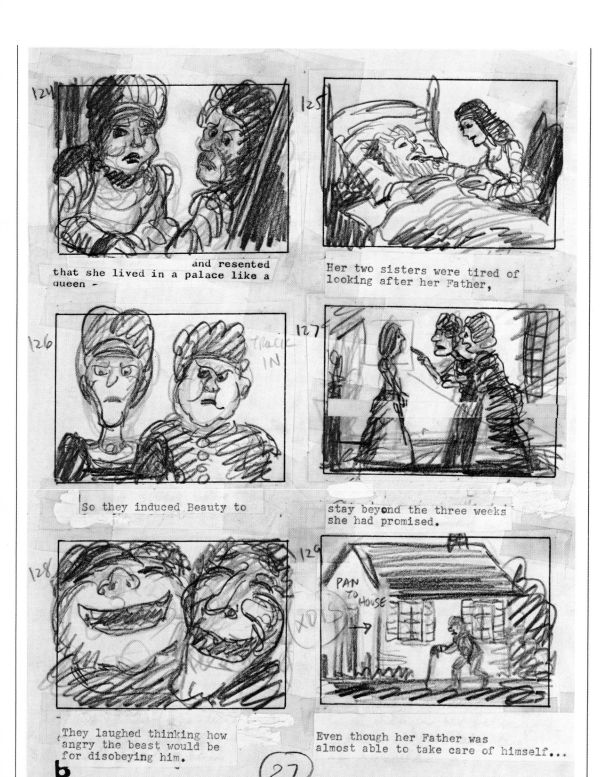

A page from the story-board of Bosustow's BEAUTY AND THE BEAST: storyboard drawings are usually done in a rough, loose style—the visual equivalent of shorthand.

COURTESY OF BOSUSTOW ENTERTAINMENT

124

125

and resented that she lived in a palace like a queen -

Her two sisters were tired of looking after her Father,

126

127 TRACK IN

So they induced Beauty to

stay beyond the three weeks she had promised.

128

129 PAN TO HOUSE

They laughed thinking how angry the beast would be for disobeying him.

Even though her Father was almost able to take care of himself...

b

27

4. The Storyboard/Story Sketch Artist

The storyboard artist is responsible for doing the drawings used to make up the storyboard for the film. The storyboard was invented at the Disney studio to help bring structure to the sprawling chaotic cartoons of the 1920's. It proved so effective as a tool that most Hollywood features and all television commercials are now storyboarded before production begins.

A storyboard may be done on large sheets of paper, or may consist of many small drawings pinned to a corkboard. A drawing is used to demonstrate what each shot within each scene will look like; lines of dialogue and/or descriptions of the action accompany each drawing. During planning meetings, the drawings may be rearranged or replaced as the various artists refine their ideas.

Animator John Canemaker makes point while presenting a storyboard.

The storyboard gives the director an overview of the film at a glance. Each shot can be studied on its own and in relation to the rest of the film. If too many shots are overly similar—say, too many close-ups of characters' heads—the film will become uninteresting visually. If the shots and scenes do not relate to each other properly, the results may be a confused, disorderly film. The director and *scene planners* work from the storyboard sketches when they do their layout drawings.

Gary Goldman, of Don Bluth Productions, concisely explained the value of the storyboard: "We save an enormous amount of money by preplanning everything and doing the editing at the storyboard stage. That way, we don't waste effort on something we don't use."

5. The Designer

The designer is responsible for the physical look of the film. Working with the director, the designer determines the color schemes of the various scenes and the appearance of the characters. A prerequisite for this job is a thorough understanding of the principles of visual design and color harmony.

Maurice Noble, who designed many of the Warner Brothers cartoons, described his job to film historian Joe Adamson thusly: "I design in *motion.* If you have a panoramic shot, it's a series of areas that are exposed to the eye as they pass through . . . your overall total has to balance out to be an interesting eye experience . . . a visual composition in motion. And this is purely done by the use of color and space relationships, accents in patterns of forms, and so forth."

The designer also works on the *model sheets.* A model sheet shows the animators how the character is constructed and looks from various angles and with different expressions. It enables the artists who will draw the character to maintain a uniform appearance and proportions. Usually the characters are based on structures of spheres, ovoids, and cubes. The animators *rough* in these basic shapes, which are easy to keep in perspective, then refine and modify them into the forms of the character's body.

① START WITH
AN OVAL SHAPE
FOR THE SKULL

② PLACE EYELINE
AT HALFWAY

③ EARFOLD LINES
UP WITH EYELINE

④ DO NOT LET
THE TWO HAIR
GROUPINGS GET
OUT OF HAND SO AS
TO DESTROY THE
SHAPE OF THE
SKULL

⑤

A SPIT
CURL COVERS
THE INSERTION
OF THE EAR

MRS. BRISBY CONST.
MODEL SHEET

EARS SLANT
IN AND UPWARD
FROM BASE OF
THE SKULL

EYE SLANTS
UPWARD

ACHIEVE
A FEELING OF
UPWARD SWEEP
MOTION IN
THE HAIR

WHISKERS GROW
OUTWARD IN A
RADIAL MOTION
JUST BELOW
NOSE.

THE BOW
HAS ONE
SIDE SHORT
AND ONE
LONG.

CAPE CAN
OVERLAP IN
FRONT

A model sheet from THE SECRET OF NIMH explains how the character, Mrs. Brisby, is constructed.

A model sheet for Hootie Owl, a character in Hanna-Barbera's HEIDI'S SONG; a finished cel shows the character's final form.

97-14 "HEIDI'S SONG"
RUFF STUDIES HOOTIE
©1979 Hanna Barbera Prod. Inc.
11/5

The visual style of the film may be created spontaneously by the designer and director, or they may choose to emulate a particular artist or style. For Disney's SLEEPING BEAUTY, Eyvind Earle adapted the look of 15th century French illuminated manuscripts to capture a rich fairy-tale feeling. For UPA's striking version of Edgar Allan Poe's THE TELL-TALE HEART, designer Paul Julian evoked the stark style of scenic designer Eugene Berman, with fragments of architecture and tattered curtains silhouetted against a dark sky.

6. The Voice Artist

While live-action dialogue is recorded during the filming or dubbed in later, the sound track for an animated film is recorded *before* the drawings are done. It is used by the animators as a timing device: once the artist knows that it takes a charcter 5 seconds to say "hello," the number of drawings needed to fill that time will also be known (24 frames per second by time in seconds).

The director of the film works with the voice artists in much the same way a live-action director works with actors and actresses, explaining the scene and coaching them to interpret the lines the way he or she wants them.

Sometimes the voice is used to help determine the look of the characters; Baloo the bear and Bagheera the panther, in Disney's THE JUNGLE BOOK, bore more than a passing resemblance to Phil Harris and Sebastian Cabot who provided their voices. But most animation voices are done by a relatively small number of actors and actresses, most of whom have had training in radio. Specialists like Mel Blanc (Bugs Bunny, Daffy Duck, Barney Rubble, Sylvester), Dawes Butler

Two examples of styling a film: British illustrator Alan Aldridge designed the intricate castle for FAERIES using the imagery of artists like Breughal and Bosch.

Painter Eyvind Earle, shown at work at the Disney Studio, adapted the look of 15th century French illuminated manuscripts for SLEEPING BEAUTY.

(Huckleberry Hound, Yogi Bear, Snagglepuss), and June Foray (Rocky the Flying Squirrel, Natasha Fatale, Witch Hazel, Broomhilda) do dozens of voices with a wide range of accents and ages. A voice artist may do several characters in a single production, play scenes with himself, and answer his own questions.

Once the director is satisfied with the performances and the voices have been recorded (sound effects and music are usually added later, unless the animation has to be timed to the music for a dance sequence), the director analyzes the sound track and prepares *exposure sheets*. An exposure sheet is a frame-by-frame breakdown of the sounds and actions of the film. These sheets tell the animator exactly how many frames (and, therefore, how many drawings) are required to accomplish a specific movement. If *lip-sync* dialogue is being used in the film, the exposure sheets will list the number of frames the sounds require in each word.

7. The Layout Artist/Scene Planner

On a large-scale production, such as a feature or a weekly television series, there will be artists who work from the storyboard sketches and the director's notes to do layout drawings or *scene plans*. These artists draft the physical appearance of the scene: where the character will enter the scene, how it will move through the scene, where it will exit, etc. If there are camera moves, such as pans and trucks, the scene planner must calculate the rates of movement and make sure the drawings and backgrounds involved are the correct dimensions. The drawings and notes of the scene planner provide a guide for the animator when developing a particular scene.

8. The Production Supervisor

A studio may have a production supervisor, an assistant to the producer who deals with day-to-day administrative problems. The production supervisor is usually in charge of ordering supplies, from pencils and animation paper to raw film stock. If the studio does not have an accounting department, this person may also handle routine financial matters.

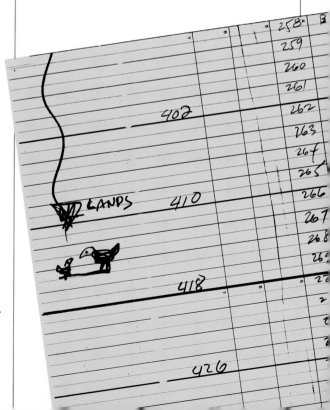

9. The Background Artist

The background artist's title is self-
explanatory: he or she creates the artwork
that serves as a setting for the animated action.
This artist works closely with the designer so
that the background style matches the general
look of the film. A rounded, realistically
shaded Disney character would look out of
place in the highly colored and stylized
deserts of the ROAD RUNNER films. However,
the colors and style of the backgrounds must
not be too close to those of the characters or
they will blend together and the action will be
lost.

Traditionally, animation backgrounds have
been done in watercolor, gouache (an opaque
watercolor used by designers), or tempera.
More recently, backgrounds have been rendered in a variety of media: pastels, pen and
ink, colored markers, and collages made from
wallpaper samples or pages from magazines.

Often the artist will do a series of *overlays*
painted on cels and coordinated with the
background to give an illusion of depth and
allow a character to move within a setting,
rather than just in front of it. If the background is a watercolor of a forest floor with
great tree trunks, the artist may add an overlay of foreground elements, such as ferns. The
cels of the character are placed between the
background and the overlay, so that the character seems to move in front of the tree
trunks but behind the ferns. If the scene is to
be photographed on a *multiplane* camera, the
artist will paint the overlays on sheets of glass.

10. The Animator

Animators or *key animators* must be actors as
well as artists. They must understand not
only the physical aspects of a character's
movements, but the elements of psychology
and personality that will make the character
move in its own unique way. Watching animators talk is usually entertaining. Their
expressions, gestures, and speaking style tend
to be vivid because they experiment and
demonstrate how characters move as they
work out the action in front of mirrors and for
each other.

After conferring with the director about a
scene, the animator sits down at the drawing
table with model sheets, layout drawings, the
exposure sheets and, very often, a tape of the
sound track. Now comes the challenge of
making the character do what the scene
requires.

Every motion in an animated film is created from a series of drawings, each one slightly different from the one preceding and following it. The key animator, however, rarely does the entire sequence of drawings. The title "key animator" comes from the fact that this person does the key drawings for each action: the extreme poses of each movement, the wildest exaggerations of expression, the points at which weight shifts and changes in balance occur or a turn begins. The key animator may invent bits of "business" to emphasize the personality of the character performing the action, such as having a small boy twist his cap while explaining how the window got broken or a dowager arch her wrist as she reaches to pick up a teacup.

The animator checks the drawings by flipping through them over and over until satisfied with the smoothness of the movement. Each drawing is then numbered, notes are made

concerning how many drawings go between each of the extremes and the rate at which the movement is being performed, and the scene is passed on to the assistant animator.

11. The Assistant Animator or In-Betweener

Assistant animators are usually young artists, still learning their art. Virtually every major animator and animation director began as an assistant. The assistant studies the drawings the animator has sent, consults with him or her, and then does the drawings that go "in between." If the animator has done drawings 1, 2, 7, 10, 15, and 16 of a lion opening his mouth to roar, the assistant must do drawings 3, 4, 5, 6, 8, 9, 11, 12, 13, and 14. Both the assistant and the animator will check the movements by flipping the stack of drawings.

When they are satisfied with the rendering of a scene, the drawings will be shot on videotape or black-and-white film. This process is known as a *pencil test* because the original pencil drawings are filmed. The pencil test is carefully studied; each movement is checked for timing, smoothness, weight, and emphasis. Any mistakes will have to be redrawn. If the movements are satisfactory, the drawings are sent to the clean-up artist.

12. The Clean-up Artist

Animators' drawings are usually rough and sketchy. They are done quickly to capture the spontaneity of the artists' thoughts. When doing a drawing, the animator is concerned with delineating the essence of a movement, not with doing a fine rendering. Also, animators use construction lines—systems of circles, blocks, and tubes—to ensure the character's proportions remain constant and that the figure stays in perspective. (Some animators at Disney used to trace around a quarter for Mickey Mouse's head and a nickel for his ears.)

Animator Glen Keane working at his animation table: weeks of drawing may be required to complete the animation of a single scene.

A rough drawing from one of the Chevron dinosaur commercials by Kurtz and Friends: the circles help the animators place the main masses.

The same drawing after clean-up.

An inked cel of the dinosaurs ready to be painted.

The clean-up artist takes these drawings and traces them, turning the loose, broken lines into a single elegant outline, but always attempting to retain the spontaneity and vigor of the original. The clean-up artist must have a sharp eye for detail; the character must look exactly the same in every drawing. If the pudgy little man has three hairs on the top of his head on the model sheet, there must be three hairs on his head in every finished drawing.

13. The Inkers and Painters

Next, the cleaned-up drawings are transferred to sheets of clean acetate called *"cels."* They are either traced by hand by an inker, using a fine brush or pen, or are transferred mechanically by a special photocopying machine. The backs of the cels are then painted by painters according to precise color models that show what color is to be used where on each character. Special acrylic paints that adhere to the surface of the acetate are required.

The color model shows the painters what colors to use on each area of each image.

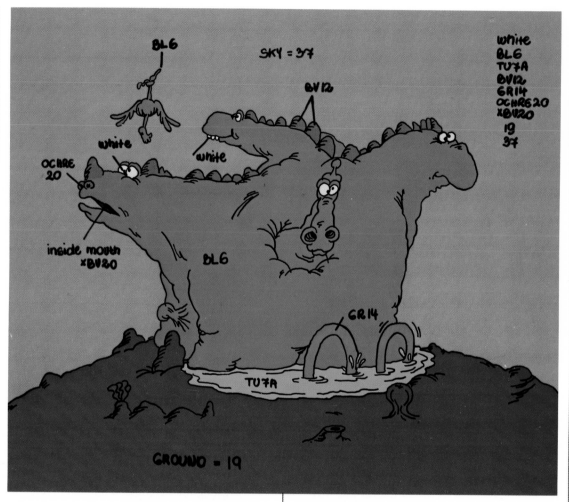

Cel painting is an exact process. The paint must be puddled onto the surface so that no brush marks show, because they would appear as streaks on the screen. The edge of the paint must touch each line so that no gaps show, but it must never go over the lines. Sometimes special effects are needed such as airbrushing, dry brushing, translucent paints, or colored inks. Some of the cels showing fairies in the *Nutcracker Suite* sequence of FANTASIA took 5 hours apiece to ink and paint, but appeared on the screen for only one twenty-fourth of a second. Because the ink and paint process is highly labor intensive, it is very expensive.

"About 20 years ago, when you wanted to calculate the cost of ink and paint for a film, you took the cost of the animation and divided it in half," says Judi Cassell, who maintains an ink and paint service in Los Angeles. "Today, you take the cost of the animation and double it."

14. The Checker

The checker is the quality-control agent of animation, ensuring that everything for each scene has been done correctly before it is filmed. The cels are counted and the exposure sheets are checked to make sure that all the necessary art is there and that it is correctly labeled and numbered. This individual makes sure the cels are in the order in which they will be photographed and examines each cel to make sure the colors are correct, checking them against the color models. If a painter has made a mistake and colored a dog's tongue the wrong shade of pink, the checker must catch the error and see that it is corrected. A small area of the wrong color seen on the screen for only a twenty-fourth of a second may sound trivial, but that error will produce an annoying flicker.

The checker also makes certain that the correct backgrounds are with the cels. If special artwork is required, such as long backgrounds for a pan, the measurements are checked and the beginning and ending points are clearly labeled for the camera operator. When the checker is satisfied that everything is as it should be, the scene is sent to be filmed.

15. The Camera Operator

The techniques and equipment needed to photograph an animated film are described in detail in Chapter 4. It is a painstaking and difficult process because the smallest error will be magnified on the screen. A professional operator may be able to shoot a minute's worth of animation in a few hours, depending on the difficulty of the scene. For an amateur filmmaker or student, shooting even a few seconds of film can be a nerve-wracking experience. The need for precision, utter cleanliness (dust particles on the artwork will be visible in the finished film), and attention to detail for each of the many, many frames quickly takes a toll on patience and neck muscles.

When the photography is completed, the exposed film is sent to a laboratory for processing.

16. The Editor

Because so much planning and checking is done before the filming, there is usually very little editing to be done on an animated film. In some studios, the editor does little more than to remove any mistakes made by the camera operator, makes sure the focus and exposure are correct, and synchronizes the sound track and the visuals. On a feature film, however, individual scenes may have to be shortened or altered to maintain the correct pace or tone for the film. Short films rarely require this sort of work.

Once the editor's work is completed, the film and the sound track are sent to the laboratory where they are combined. Prints can be struck for distribution and viewing in theatres around the world.

4

The Animation Stand

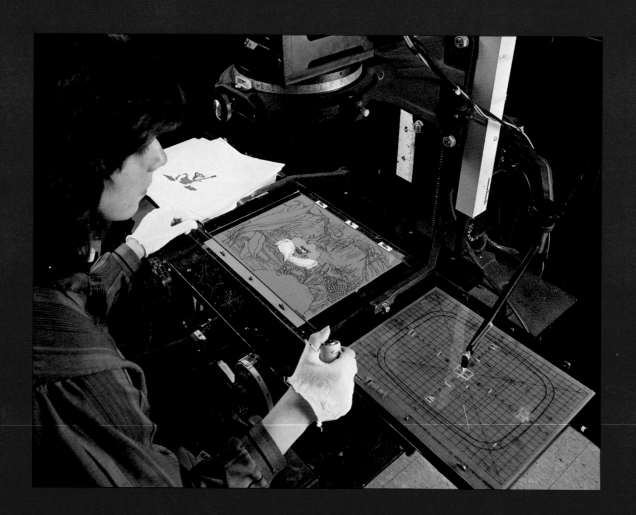

Photographing an animated film is a precise and delicate task. Twenty-four exposures, taken one frame at a time, are needed for every second of screen time, or almost 1,500 exposures for every minute. The artwork must be kept scrupulously clean throughout this recording process, as particles of dust or fingerprints will show in the finished film. Naturally, smoking, eating, and drinking are forbidden in the area during the photography. Animation camera rooms are so clean they often resemble hospital rooms. It is in these spotless environments that the painstaking photography is done.

1. Field Size and the Field Chart

Animation paper and cels are cut to an industry standard size of 12½″ x 10½″; within each sheet is an area 12″ x 8¾″ called a *12-field*. These dimensions represent the largest area that can be photographed by a standard animation camera. (The remaining space is used for borders and the punch—see the

photograph.) This area is divided into concentric rectangles in one-inch increments: An 11-field measures 11″ x 8″ and so on, down to the smallest standard size, the 2-field (2″ x 1½″). While the paper and cels remain the same size, the area within them that is used and photographed does not.

Camera operators, layout artists, directors, and animators all keep track of the field sizes with a *field chart.*

Field sizes allow the director and the animator considerable flexibility. If the director wants the camera to move in on a close-up of an object in the frame, the camera operator can be instructed to go from a 12-field to a 7-field. This will give the effect of a truck into a close-up more easily than drawing the movement in perspective could. An animator also may prefer to draw a character within a certain area because the pencil strokes are more comfortable for the hand and wrist, so the drawings are done on a 10-field instead of a 12-field area and the camera shoots at that field size. In the resulting film, the characters will fill the frame as completely as if they had been drawn larger on a larger field.

2. The Punch

One of the first problems animators faced was keeping their drawings in *register:* Every element in the drawing must appear in the same place on each sheet of paper. Winsor McCay used a crosshatch mark in each corner and placed the pieces of paper in a special holder. It was Raoul Barré who first devised the system of punching the paper and placing *pegs* on the animators' tables, the inkers' desks, and the camera stand—a system still in use today.

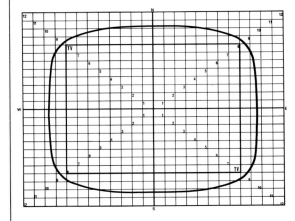

Currently, the Acme punch is used in most west coast studios, while the Oxberry punch is preferred on the east coast and in Europe. A few studios even have their own punch design. Which punch is used is unimportant, so long as all the people in the studio—directors, animators, layout artists, painters, and camera operators—use the same one.

3. The Stand

The *animation stand* resembles a heavy steel table with a *crane arm* rising from the back to support the camera. Because it is cheaper and easier to create certain moves and effects like *trucks, pans, rotations, tilts, dissolves,* and *fades* by moving the camera and/or the artwork than it is to draw them, the entire assembly is designed to be flexible and responsive to very small adjustments. The animation stand is also designed to be extremely stable because the slightest movement of the artwork while it is actually being photographed would be visible as a blur in the finished film. The need to reconcile these two very different requirements has produced a highly sophisticated piece of equipment. Like typewriters and cars manufactured by different companies, animation stands of different manufacturers have special features and unique details, but they all share certain common features. This chapter examines and describes a "typical" animation stand and its functions.

The artwork rests on the surface of a table-like structure called the *compound.* Directly under the camera on the compound are two or four sets of peg bars that hold the artwork

(Top to bottom) The Acme punch, the Oxberry punch, and the old Disney punch: three different solutions to the problem of keeping the artwork in registration. Which punch is used on an individual production doesn't matter, but everyone involved must use the same one.

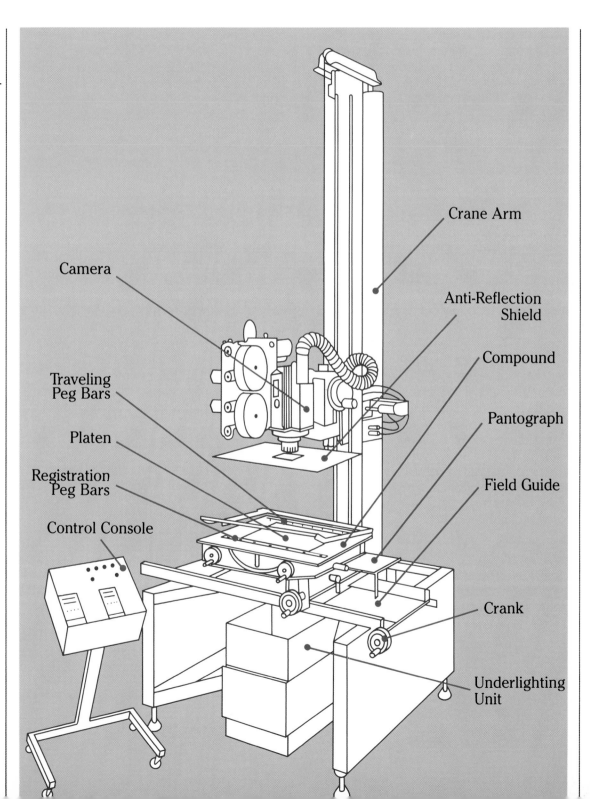

The animation stand and its basic parts. Note: The lights are usually placed on either side of the compound to light the artwork evenly.

Crane Arm

Camera

Anti-Reflection Shield

Compound

Traveling Peg Bars

Pantograph

Platen

Field Guide

Registration Peg Bars

Control Console

Crank

Underlighting Unit

while it is being photographed. Usually the background is placed on the top pegs; this keeps it in place throughout the scene while the operator changes the cels of the characters on the front pegs, which are easier to reach. The background may also be taped to the compound to ensure greater stability while long scenes are being filmed.

All the peg bars on the compound are moveable. They are controlled by dials marked in tenths or hundredths of an inch. This system is used to create pan moves and is called a set of traveling peg bars. If Bugs Bunny is supposed to walk down the street towards the right side of the screen, it will be filmed this way: The operator places a long background of the street scene on the top bars and keeps repeating a *cycle* of cels of Bugs' walk on the bottom pegs. Before each frame is photographed, the background is moved a fraction of an inch to the left by adjusting the correct dial. Each movement will probably only be a few hundredths of an inch—even a speeding fire truck wouldn't move more than about one-tenth of an inch per frame. When the results are projected, Bugs will seem to be walking down the street with his usual speed and nonchalance. The dials controlling the panning peg bars can be locked in place when the artwork is supposed to remain still, to prevent accidental jolts.

The panning peg bars can only move the artwork horizontally or, if the camera is rotated 90 degrees, vertically. Sometimes the camera has to move on a diagonal, say from a 4-field in the lower left corner to a 4-field in the upper right corner. To accomplish this, the entire compound is moved on two sets of worm gears. Like the panning peg bars, these gears are attached to delicately calibrated control dials. These dials control the movement of the compound in either north-south or east-west directions. The *pantograph,* a pointer positioned over a *field guide,* shows the operator the exact position of the compound under the camera. Because it is very difficult to move the compound in small even amounts in two directions every frame, this sort of off-center movement is rarely used.

Attached to the compound is a pair of hinged metal arms that hold a sheet of heavy glass, slightly larger than a 12-field, called the *platen.* The platen holds the artwork in place while it is actually being photographed. The platen holds the cels flat against the background so they cannot cast shadows. A foam pad on top of the compound absorbs the pressure. (The camera moves described above are done *between* exposures: The artwork must be absolutely still while it is photographed.)

4. Lighting

Unlike live-action, the lighting for animation photography is extremely simple—it is used only to illuminate the artwork for the camera. Effects usually generated by the lights, like shadows, are done by the animators and painters on the artwork itself. A photoflood lamp is placed on either side of the compound at a 45-degree angle to the surface of the artwork. The standard studio flood lamp is rated at 3000 K, which is compatible with most 16 mm and 35 mm color films.

For certain special effects, *bottom lighting* may be used. The pad on which the artwork normally rests is removed and replaced with a sheet of Plexiglas. Lights placed under the compound shine up through the glass and the artwork. To create stars, for example, a cel with random splotches of paint is placed over the Plexiglas. A black card pierced with small pinholes goes over the cel. When this arrangement is filmed, the light shines through the pinholes and registers on the film as tiny points of colored light, giving the illusion of stars against the black of space.

5. The Camera

An animation camera is essentially a motion picture camera with single-frame and reverse capabilities. The film gauge (super 8, 16 mm, or 35 mm) and the make of the camera depend on the needs and resources of the studio or individual who owns it, but the reverse and single-frame features are essential.

The camera is mounted in a ring of heavy steel that is marked in degrees, so it can be turned for *rotations* and *tilts*. A rotation would be used when Yogi Bear is trying to show off his skills as a flying ace and manages to turn the plane upside down. The terrified Boo-Boo looks through the windshield and sees the sky where the ground should be and vice versa. To shoot this scene, the operator places the artwork with the ground at the bottom of the compound; then turns the camera 180 degrees and films the upside-down sequence. When the plane rights itself, the camera is turned a few degrees before taking each exposure until it is back in the normal position. The audience, looking through the windshield with Boo-Boo, sees the ground slowly return to its normal position and everyone breathes a sigh of relief. A tilt is simply a partial rotation.

The camera can also be moved up and down the crane arm by a small motor; it is too heavy to be moved by gears and knobs like the peg bars. This type of camera move is called a *truck*. If the scene calls for the camera to truck in on a close-up, the beginning and ending field sizes will be noted on the exposure sheet, along with the number of frames allotted for the move and how far the camera should be moved each frame. The distance will be marked on the crane arm in tiny increments, usually drawn on a piece of graph paper and taped into place. The camera will be moved a fraction of an inch before each exposure is taken. Like pans, trucks must be done in tiny equal increments every frame or the result will be uneven and jerky looking.

Another effect achieved by the camera operator is a *fade*. By adjusting the camera aperture between frames, fade-outs (by slowly closing the aperture) or fade-ins (by slowly opening the aperture) can be created. The camera's reverse capability is used when shooting a *dissolve,* which is a fade-in superimposed over a fade-out. When Mickey Mouse plays magician, he may want to turn his top hat into a vase of flowers. Checking the exposure sheet, the operator films the scene with the hat in place but closes the aperture 2 percent more for each frame. With the shutter closed, the film is then wound back to where the fade-out started and the cel of the hat is replaced by the cel of the vase. Now the scene is shot again, opening the aperture by 2 percent each frame. On the screen, the hat will be miraculously replaced by the vase of flowers: Mickey's trick works!

A layout drawing for a combination rotation and pan: the camera begins at the far right, turned perpendicular to the edge of the paper; as it moves along the pan, it slowly rotates 90° until it reaches its final position.

The finished artwork
for the same sequence.

A similar technique is used for another effect, *multipass*. As the name suggests, multipass involves exposing the same film two, three, or more times at various light levels: each exposure is a "pass." This process is used to produce a translucent image—a shadow, a ghost, a filmy cloud in a sunrise. It is costly to use multipass because the positions of the artwork must be matched with almost microscopic precision for each of the exposures. Also, because the same film is being used over and over, mistakes cannot be edited out. If an error is made on any one of the passes, the operator must go back to the beginning and start over. Often, a mistake is not noticed until the workprint, so it's important to retain the artwork and a record of methods used.

A striking example of the use of multipass was seen in the television special FAERIES, when the hero, Oisin, fought the Faerie King's evil shadow. On the first pass, the background and the cels of Oisin were shot with the aperture fully open. On the second pass, the cels of the shadow were added to the scene, but the aperture was partially closed. This produced a ghostly, shadow-like creature that changed the color of things it moved in front of, but did not obliterate them. The audience could both see and see through the shadow.

6. The Camera Operator

The camera operator who has to execute all these complicated moves and techniques while sitting in a small room filled with hot lights needs the patience of Job and the dexterity of a brain surgeon. The operator sits at the compound with the artwork for a given

A combination truck and pan: the camera begins with a close-up of the pie, moves back (truck), then moves over the landscape to the right (pan), following the trail of the steam.

The Shadow Monster from FAERIES: multipass techniques were used to create its filmy appearance. The background and the other characters were photographed once normally; the film was rewound and exposed again at a certain percentage after the cels of the shadow were added to the scene.

scene on a table to one side. The exposure sheet is checked and the appropriate background is placed on the compound. Next, after removing any particles of dust with a special brush or antistatic device, the correct cel is laid over the background.

On many stands, the shutter and the platen are attached to foot pedals, freeing the operator's hands to change artwork. The platen swings down; the shutter clicks: a single frame of film has been exposed. The platen swings up. The operator removes the cel, checks the exposure sheet, and puts on the next cel. Again, the platen swings down and another frame is exposed.

The operator's job becomes even more difficult when camera moves are involved in combination—a pan and a truck, together, for example, or a dissolve and a truck. Adjustments must be made every frame, and the operator must remember, in the middle of changing cels, whether or not the peg bars have been adjusted for that exposure. The new computerized animation stands are useful here: The computer can be preprogrammed to perform all the moves in a scene more quickly and accurately than a human operator can. The operator just changes the artwork and triggers the shutter. Although a computerized animation stand can cost well over $100,000, it may prove to be a good investment for a studio because of the time and effort it can save.

A spokesperson for a Chicago studio confirms, "The computerized stand saves us a lot of time. We don't have to think about the camera the way we used to—at the design stages we always had to be aware of the time and costs involved in shooting. With our computerized setup we can do things easily, that would be nearly impossible to do by hand."

7. The Multiplane Camera

The multiplane camera is a special animation stand used for shots where an illusion of great depth is desired. It was created at the Disney Studio in the mid-1930's, largely from designs by Ub Iwerks, and first used in THE OLD MILL in 1937. The sense of depth is achieved by painting various background and foreground elements on sheets of glass (cels can be used on specific levels for action) which are placed in holders several inches apart. The lighting for each level and the relative rates of pans and trucks must be carefully calculated.

The multiplane stand is very large—the size of a small room in some cases—and expensive to build and use. Only the Disney Studio has made extensive use of it. The apparent depth of multiplane shots gives a richness that strengthens the feeling of three-dimensionality in many of the Disney features. The handsome vistas of the great forest in the opening of BAMBI were shot on the multiplane camera, as was the sequence in SLEEPING BEAUTY at Aurora's christening when the camera seems to move past the lofty Gothic pillars of the main hall of King Stephan's castle.

8. The Video Animation Stand

A persistent problem for animators was the delay between when they finished their drawings and when they could look at the pencil tests. Usually, about 3 days were required for the drawings to be shot and the film processed: By that time, the animators had forgotten details of what they were trying to convey through their drawings. The ideas got "cold" during the wait.

Animation on videotape: at an early stage in the production, an animator can shoot rough drawings and instantly play back the tape to check movement and determine if any changes are necessary.

Bruce Lyon and John Lamb solved this problem in the late 1970's when they introduced the Lyon-Lamb Video Animation System, which was awarded an Oscar for technical achievement in 1980. The video animation system resembles a conventional black-and-white porta-pack setup, except that the recorder moves the tape in one twenty-fourth of a second intervals each time a drawing is shot. The real advantage of the system is its instant replay. As soon as the last drawing has been shot, the tape can be rewound and watched. The animators can look at their drawings in motion while the ideas are still fresh in their minds.

Almost every major studio now has at least one video system for pencil tests. The success of the invention has led other manufacturers to market similar setups. The technology of these systems is rapidly becoming more sophisticated, as features like video memories and edit modes are developed.

However, a video system may cost $10,000 or more, which places it out of the range of many independent filmmakers and schools. These artists continue to shoot their pencil tests on inexpensive black-and-white stock. Because fewer and fewer labs handle black-and-white film these days, some animators develop their own tests the way photographers develop still pictures. The chemicals are readily available and inexpensive, and the results are quite satisfactory.

Because they are simple tests, seen only by the artists involved in the project, pencil tests do not have to be high-quality prints. Visibility of the image is sufficient. Usually, the artists won't even bother to strike a print of the test, but will just project the original. No one would do this with a finished film, because each projection can scratch or damage the film; but for a pencil test, the stock lasts long enough to accomplish the purpose of the test.

The demand for special effects in science-fiction films has caused many live-action filmmakers to use animation cameras, techniques, and operators to achieve the look they seek. Live-action filmmakers are learning what animators have known for a long time: A skilled animation camera operator using good equipment and the correct techniques can give a director more complete control of the image than can be achieved with conventional live-action methods.

Independent
Animators

Since animation emerged as an art form, there has been a dichotomy between animation as a collaborative studio product and animation as an expression of a personal artistic vision. Studio animation is one of the few truly collective art forms, with dozens of artists all contributing to each film. But some artists are uncomfortable operating within the structure of a studio that needs to produce films that have commercial appeal. While the work of these independent animators is not widely known, it occupies an important place in the history of frame-by-frame filmmaking.

In many ways, Winsor McCay can be seen as the first of the independent animators. He was interested in perfecting an art form: Unlike many early animators, he never showed any interest in founding a studio. He preferred to do the drawings for his films himself, using assistants only for routine tasks like tracing backgrounds. The smooth, carefully timed animation of his films is strikingly different from the stiff formula products of the early cartoon studios. In fact, McCay was outspoken in his dislike of these commercial films, which he saw as a debauchment of his art.

Since that time, many artists have followed McCay's lead, striving to realize a personal vision of what animation can and should be. With the demise of most of the large Hollywood studios, which had been centers of research and creativity in the late 1950's, independent animators have come to play an increasingly important role. It is in their films that most of the interesting and exciting experimentation has been done, especially in recent decades. New styles and subjects have been explored in ways that are not feasible for commercial studios.

This freedom to experiment is not without its drawbacks. Both the audience and the market for experimental animated films are limited. A 3- or 5-minute short that may represent a year of work and thousands of dollars in expenses cannot command a rental fee of more than about $25. To survive, independent animators support themselves in a number of ways. They may work in studios during the day and do their own films at night, or they may work for commercial houses on a free-lance basis. They may teach filmmaking or take a part-time job in areas unrelated to their art. Only a few are able to support themselves through their filmmaking.

This chapter examines the work of seven interesting and important animators who have chosen to go their own way and make their own films outside of a studio setting.

John Canemaker:
The Animator as Historian

Animators are usually depicted as tongue-tied people who express themselves through their drawings because they are uncomfortable using words. This stereotype certainly doesn't apply to John Canemaker. In addition to being a well-respected animator, Canemaker is one of the world's foremost authorities on the history and aesthetics of animation. While his interest in animation has been lifelong, he became a film historian by a rather roundabout path.

"I began making animated films when I was a teenager," he recalls. "There were no schools teaching animation then, and if you looked the subject up in the library, all you would find was Robert Field's book on Disney and Preston Blair's book on basic drawing techniques. Occasionally the 'Disneyland' television program featured animation, and Walter Lantz gave little speeches on 'The Woody Woodpecker Show,' but that was it.

"So I dropped animation, moved to New York City and became an actor. In 1971, I decided to put myself through school with the money I was earning as an actor. I went to Marymount Manhattan College, where I got my B.A., and to New York University, where I got my M.F.A. in film. I took evening classes in animation at the School of Visual Arts, as a sort of refresher."

In 1973, a teacher at Marymount sent Canemaker to the Disney studio in Burbank, California, to do research at their newly opened archive. A number of the original animators were still there, and Canemaker interviewed many of them. After his rather extensive research paper was completed, he began to "spin off" articles from it. His reputation as an animation historian started to grow; he did more interviews with pioneers like J. R. Bray and Otto Messmer, which led to more articles.

To date he has written more than 100 articles, which have appeared in a number of journals, including *Film Comment, Print, Horizon, Millimeter,* and *Film News.* In 1977, he published *The Animated Raggedy Ann & Raggedy Andy: An Intimate Look at the Art of Animation,* which remains one of the best books available on studio animation. He created two excellent documentaries: REMEMBERING WINSOR MCCAY (1976), which combined clips of McCay's animation and an interview with McCay's assistant, John Fitzsimmons, and OTTO MESSMER AND FELIX THE CAT (1977), in which he revealed the little-known story of how Messmer created the first animated cartoon star. Canemaker also wrote and hosted three programs on animation for CBS-TV's "Camera Three."

THE WIZARD'S SON, Canemaker's whimsical parable of the conflict between the aspirations of parents and their children: The wizard wants his son to follow him in his profession; the son wants to be a musician.

A strip of film from THE WIZARD'S SON (1981) with the title character.

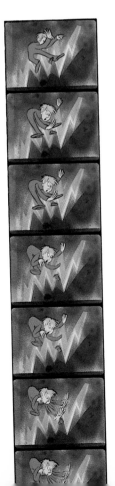

"The reason the history of animation has been so poorly documented is because of a lack of interest and a lack of information," he explains. "Historically, it has been very hard to get to see the experimental work done in animation; it's still hard to see today, only at a slightly lesser degree. The greater history of animation is still largely unknown to the general public. A few writers and historians are beginning to explore it, but there are only a few of us."

He feels this growing interest in animation's past is due in part to the emergence of a new and larger audience for animated films:

"I think a large part of this new audience is coming from the schools. Animation is being widely taught for the first time: Virtually every major college has at least a basic class in frame-by-frame filmmaking, as do many high schools and elementary schools. There's much more information about animation available now than there was just 10 or 15 years ago, and people are taking advantage of its availability. Most of the people who are becoming involved in the art form received their introduction to it in the schools."

But recently Canemaker has been writing less and animating more. In addition to films for "Sesame Street" and a number of commercials, including one for the road tour of THE ROCKY HORROR SHOW, he has made a number of personal films. CONFESSIONS OF A STAR DREAMER (1978), an examination of an aspiring actress's fantasies about success that features a variety of animation techniques, was selected for the National Endowment for the Arts Short Film Showcase. His most recent film, THE WIZARD'S SON (1981), deals with conflicts between a parent's expectations and a child's personal goals. Canemaker was also recently involved in a project that brought animation to Broadway in the popular musical *Woman of the Year*.

In the original script, Sam Craig (Harry Guardino) was a sports writer, but his occupation was changed to newspaper cartoonist in the production. For the number "So What Else is New?", Guardino does a duet with an animated version of his comic strip's star, a black-and-white cat named Katz. Guardino and the orchestra do the song live, while the cat is rear projected. The conductor has a click track, so he can keep the duet in sync.

"At first, they just wanted slides of the character," comments Canemaker. "Then they decided he should be animated. Michael Sporn produced and directed, and I did the animation: We had a 3-week schedule to get it done and up to Boston for the show's tryouts, which was insane. This project represents the first extensive use of animation in a Broadway show, and the audience reactions have been quite favorable."

Canemaker more recently completed work on some experimental animation for George Roy Hill's film based on the best-selling novel, *The World According to Garp*. But despite his success with the medium, Canemaker retains the concern of a critic and historian for the direction animation seems to be taking in America.

"Animation is in a difficult period of prolonged adolescence," he remarks wryly. "The work being done at Disney is definitely child-oriented, although they use principles that are truly universal; they could be applied to any style or story. On the other hand is the childishly oriented stuff, like Bakshi's work or HEAVY METAL. There's no place today for wit, sophistication, or maturity, especially maturity in content. Technique is one thing, but it must be put to good use.

A drawing (top) and cel with background from CONFESSIONS OF A STAR DREAMER (1978). These pieces, along with the example on page 88, demonstrate Canemaker's use of diverse artistic styles.

"I think the fragments of THE TEMPEST that George Dunning completed just before he died are a beacon of the future to us all—that was brilliant work. Or look at the films of the late John Hubley, films like OF STARS AND MEN or MOONBIRD. They're succinct, nonsexist, and nonpornographic—they're *adult*. They deal with mature themes that go beyond the self; for me, that is the way of the future in animation."

Larry Cuba: Of Animation and Computers

When Luke Skywalker flew his X-wing fighter down the trench of the Death Star to attack the exposed thermal exhaust port in STAR WARS, it wasn't only the Force that guided him. Larry Cuba showed him the way. The young computer animator created the plans for the Death Star that were read from Artoo Detoo's memory banks in the rebel briefing room—the only digital computer animation in the film.

While the effect was impressive, it was very different from the sort of films Cuba usually makes. One of the country's most respected computer animators, he did programming for John Whitney's ARABESQUE and has made three award-winning films of his own: FIRST FIG (1974); *3/78* (OBJECTS AND TRANSFORMATIONS); and TWO SPACE (1979). Cuba's personal films are austerely beautiful explorations of space, movement, and design, in which points of light move in complicated, cogent patterns. But it is the overwhelming popularity of STAR WARS that has drawn most of the attention to Cuba's work.

To create the appearance of the Death Star's surface in the model shots of Skywalker's flight, artists covered a 40-foot scale model of the trench with hundreds of plastic walls and towers cast from molds of six basic modules. To ensure greater variety, the modules were broken up into their component parts.

"I had an example of each module at the University of Illinois at Chicago Circle's chemistry department graphics laboratory where I was working," says Cuba, "and I digitized the modules. That is, I encoded into the computer a mathematical representation of each shape that used lines to represent their edges. I replicated and assembled the digitized modules on the surface of the trench structure to simulate the physical model. The two didn't match exactly, because I was constructing the computer model at the same time they were assembling the physical one. Then I had the computer draw a series of perspective projections of the finished trench from the point of view of a pilot flying through it."

Cuba first became interested in computer graphics while he was studying architecture as an undergraduate at Washington University in St. Louis, Missouri. In 1972, he moved to Los Angeles to study animation at CalArts, where he received his M.F.A. in 1974, and worked with the pioneer computer animator, John Whitney, Sr. He created his first film, FIRST FIG, while at CalArts. In 1977, he moved to Chicago for a year to accept an appointment as a Research Assistant with the Art Department of the University of Illinois at Chicago Circle, where he produced *3/78*. Upon his return to Los Angeles, he completed TWO SPACE, which he had begun somewhat earlier.

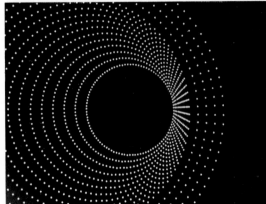

In addition to his personal films, Cuba has also worked on a number of television commercials.

"The chrome/neon look used in so many commercials that constitutes the popular image of computer animation is not likely to change much in the immediate future," he comments. "Those films are done by crews on large systems to sell a product. That's something very different from the work of an individual artist who isn't interested in dazzling chrome effects, but who is concerned with exploring ideas.

"I see my films as a form of discovery. I don't storyboard or design a film, then sit down and make a computer execute the designs—which is the way commercials are done. I enjoy not knowing what the final images will look like and discovering something that may go beyond what I could visualize. I suspect I would lose interest in a film if it were entirely predesigned; I'm really an experimenter at heart."

When he turns to the subject of the future of computer animation, Cuba speaks with enthusiasm of the possibilities for increased and novel forms of communication:

"As personal computers become cheaper, more accessible, and more popular, computer animation will become accepted as a standard form of communication: what some scientists call pictorial conversation. Photography was once a very complicated process that only a few artists practiced; now it's very common. We regularly exchange photographs as a form of communication and no one thinks anything of it. Computer animation will follow a similar pattern.

Stills from 3/78 (1978), left, and TWO SPACE (1979), right: austerely elegant patterns of white light on a black background. Cuba's personal films are characterized by understated, formal abstractions.

"Some people today react adversely to the idea of using computers in art because they're 'technology,'" he observes dryly. "Why don't they think the same thing of cameras or film? When that technology was first introduced, there were people who claimed it was 'too mechanical' to have any use in art, but now it's been completely assimilated. When home computers become common and people gain a better understanding of what computers are and what they can do, the prejudices will disappear. Computers can be frustrating, but they're not hostile. Like cars and telephones, they're becoming accepted as everyday devices, designed to make life more convenient and enjoyable."

Currently, Cuba is at work under a grant from the American Film Institute on a film for which he is developing a computer language for frame-by-frame filmmaking. Again, his enthusiasm is evident in his voice as he describes his work:

"Each of my films has been made on a different system using a different programming language. A programming language gives you the power to express some ideas, while limiting your ability to express others. I've hit those limits with every language I've used. Most languages designed for art were created by computer scientists, and they reflect their designers' assumptions about what an artist will want. Usually, they involve tactile interaction with the computer—dials, 'joy sticks,' light pens—which might be more comfortable for a traditional artist to use. These languages are of little use to me, because my work involves the exploration of mathematical and theoretical ideas. I have to develop a language of my own in which to express those ideas— I'm looking for the ultimate computer language, which is a bit like looking for the Holy Grail."

Oskar Fischinger (1900–1967): A Pioneer of Abstract Animation

Oskar Fischinger was born in Gelnhausen, Germany, on June 22, 1900, into the same generation of expressionist filmmakers as Fritz Lang and F. W. Murnau. As a boy, he studied drafting and engineering and served an apprenticeship in an organ factory, but soon left these disciplines to pursue his art.

Fischinger began his work in film around 1921 or 1922. The best known of his early films involves his wax-slicing experiments, which he started in 1923. Fischinger designed and built a machine that would remove thin slices from a block of mixed wax and clay; a frame of film was shot after each slice was taken. As the knife gradually cut through layers and lumps of the various materials, abstract patterns were formed. The easiest way to understand how these films were created is to imagine a hard-boiled egg being sliced. It begins as a small white circle that gradually grows larger; a small yellow circle appears in the center, grows larger, then smaller, then disappears; the white circle then shrinks and disappears, also.

In 1927, Fischinger moved to Berlin, where he created special effects for Fritz Lang's WOMAN IN THE MOON. At about this time, he began his STUDIES series, which occupied most of his attention until 1932. These short abstract animated films were keyed to various pieces of classical and popular music. Patterns of lines and geometric forms drawn in charcoal swoop, dip, circle, and turn to the music. Some animators have criticized Fischinger for allowing the music to dominate these films, and in their weaker moments they may seem like musical illustrations. But Fischinger's animation is fluid and elegant, and the STUDIES are striking graphic exercises.

During the mid-1930's, Fischinger did a number of advertising films that were shown in theatres. The best known of these are MURATTI MARCHES ON and MURATTI PRIVAT, which feature stop-motion animation of cigarettes marching and forming patterns in time to the sound track. At about the same time, he created one of his most popular films: COMPOSITION IN BLUE (1935). In this handsome and exhilarating work, geometric shapes of colored clay move to Otto Nicolai's *Merry Wives of Windsor* Overture.

As abstract art was anathema to the Nazi government, Fischinger found himself in a somewhat precarious position, and in late 1935 he left Germany for America, never to return. The transition proved to be a difficult one. In Europe, Fischinger had been the center of admiration in artistic circles and had won prizes in film festivals; in America, he was essentially an unknown whose aesthetic vision had little in common with the products of Hollywood studios.

During an unhappy 6-month tenure at Paramount, Fischinger created the short abstract work that eventually became known as ALLEGRETTO. It had originally been intended as an insert for THE BIG BROADCAST OF 1937, but various problems arose and the film was never used. Fischinger moved to MGM, where he completed one film: AN OPTICAL POEM (1937), synchronized to Liszt's Hungarian Rhapsody No. 2. OPTICAL POEM was released as a theatrical short to modest success, but personnel changes at the studio led to further problems and Fischinger left MGM.

Fischinger had twice approached conductor Leopold Stokowski about the possibility of working together on a film. In 1934, he proposed to do an abstract short to Stokowski's orchestral transcription of Bach's Toccata and Fugue in D Minor; in 1938, he suggested an abstract animated feature to Dvorak's New World Symphony. His ideas may have led Stokowski to suggest to Walt Disney that he make a "concert feature"—the film that ultimately became FANTASIA. In any event,

Disney hired Fischinger in 1938 to work on the Toccata and Fugue sequence.

It was a commendable attempt by both parties to try to bridge the gap between studio and independent animation, but the collaboration was not a happy one. Indeed, a clash was probably inevitable. Studio animation is inherently a collective art form, geared to pleasing a mass audience. Fischinger, like many independent filmmakers, was used to doing all the artwork for his films (he used assistants only to color his drawings) and to making all the decisions about them himself. Fischinger was extremely unhappy at Disney and stayed only about 9 months. The Toccata and Fugue sequence of FANTASIA—arguably its weakest section—does bear the marks of his influence, but it achieves neither the abstract purity of Fischinger's personal films nor the

COMPOSITION IN BLUE (1935): exhilarating stop-motion animation of geometric clay figures to "The Merry Wives of Windsor" overture by Otto Nicolai.

strength and polish of Disney's best work.

During the war years, Fischinger began working under grants from the Solomon R. Guggenheim Foundation. The first work he created for them was AMERICAN MARCH (1941), which featured images of stars and stripes moving to John Philip Sousa's "Stars and Stripes Forever." The Guggenheim trustees were so pleased with the film that Fischinger received further grants, which enabled him to buy back the rights and materials for ALLEGRETTO. At the same time, he also collaborated with Orson Welles on a number of projects. Although none of them ever came to fruition, his salary enabled him to complete another of his best-known films, RADIO DYNAMICS.

RADIO DYNAMICS and AN OPTICAL POEM are generally regarded as two of Fischinger's most successful and important works. Although the former was done on cels and the latter with paper cutouts, they share a common aesthetic. The movement of the geometric shapes, however graceful, is less important than the relationships of the shapes to each other and to the square of the frame: The emphasis is on color, form, and design. Almost any frame from either film could be blown up and framed as a nonobjective painting, reminiscent of the work of Kandinsky and Klee.

During the last decades of his life, Fischinger devoted less of his time to filmmaking and more to painting, for which he received a measure of recognition. He combined the two art forms in his last completed personal film, the celebrated MOTION PICTURE PAINTING NO. 1 (1947). Abstract designs were painted on sheets of Plexiglas material with a frame being shot after every few strokes of the

brush. When a sheet was completely covered with paint, he placed a new one over it and continued the development of his design on the fresh surface. Some critics consider MOTION PAINTING to be Fischinger's ultimate creation.

In the 1950's, Fischinger's health began to deteriorate, and he died of a heart attack in January 1967, at the age of 66. Although his films have still not received the recognition from the general public that they merit, Fischinger's place in the history of animation is secure. His work has had an enormous influence on abstract filmmakers up to the present day. His films and much of the artwork from them have been lovingly preserved by his widow, Elfriede.

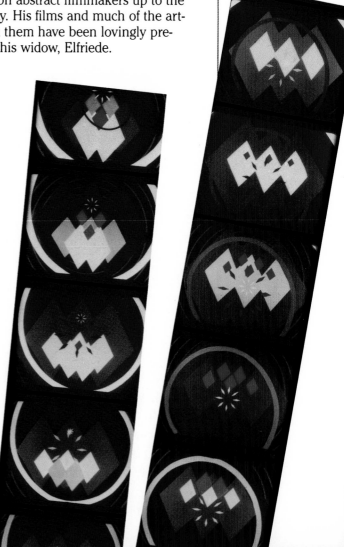

The brightly colored geometric shapes of ALLEGRETTO (1936), drawn on multiple layers of cels, were originally intended to provide an interlude in the Paramount feature, THE BIG BROADCAST OF 1937.

The films of George Griffin defy neat categorization because he has worked in so many different styles and media, and has dealt with such diverse themes. He animated patterns of black beans on white paper for his first film, RAPID TRANSIT (1969), and used paper cutouts to spoof sex roles and traditions in THE CLUB (1975). STEP PRINT (1976) is a purely abstract exploration of increasingly complex patterns of color painted on cels. LINEAGE (1979) combines drawings, cutouts, puppet animation, and live-action footage. Yet all of these very different films display the same degree of imagination, technical facility, and familiarity with the history of animation.

Unlike many independent animators, Griffin did not have a childhood affinity for animation. Although he demonstrated a talent for drawing at an early age, he pursued a standard liberal arts education.

George Griffin: Self-Reflexive Animator

STEP PRINT (1976): blocks of color that build into an increasingly complicated, abstract mosaic.

"I trace my line to find out who I am. At times the journey leads to magicians and conjurors, artistes *of the popular theater who entertain for approval and applause—a joyous and healing enterprise.*

"Then, the thread leads to the discipline and alienation of art which studies chiefly itself. The self-consciousness is bracing, cleansing even, yet I wouldn't want to live there.

"At times, these contradictory strands converge into knots, mazes, and spirals, before unravelling as gently receding horizons. Then, they burst into a multitude of impressions as evocative as scrapbooks, as honest as signatures."

—GEORGE GRIFFIN, NOTES FOR *LINEAGE*, 1979

"After graduating from Dartmouth in 1967, I moved to New York," he explains. "There I realized that I could never do things like political science as well as I could do art. My interest in art, which had remained a sort of underground stream in my life during my college career, reemerged in the form of film. Animation was the logical combination of drawing and film. Of course, the whole process wasn't as neat and orderly as that makes it sound."

Griffin got a job in an animation studio, but disliked it intensely and left after a month:

"I didn't like the assembly-line atmosphere and the hierarchical structure of the studio. I liked the scratchy, scrawly drawings the older animators would produce, and I didn't want to clean them up into a single sterile outline.

The studio was the kind of environment that would produce hard-edged, flat-colored characters with the same message—either selling cereal or telling old jokes. To be a professional there required things I found intolerable; it meant doing things in formula ways.

"I decided to make personal films instead," he adds, "films that would be my own statements. I like having the option of taking a risk in a film. The result may be a real thud, but at least there's no compromise involved."

Griffin acted on his resolve and produced more than 18 films in the 12 years between 1969 and 1981. To help support his creative work, he made commercials and taught at both New York University and Harvard.

Many of Griffin's films are highly self-reflexive. The audience is made aware they are watching a film as the process that

A poster for
VIEWMASTER (1976),
Griffin's *trope l'oeil*
study of a race.

created the images is revealed to them. In
VIEWMASTER, for example, 12 different figures
seem to follow each other around a circular
track. At the end of the film, the camera pulls
back to reveal that what the viewer has seen
is not a linear succession of images, but a circular drawing with the figures positioned
around the rim, like the numbers on a clock.
The illusion of movement was created by
slowly turning the circle as it was photographed.

"Film is an illusion, a trick; one of a battery
of tricks, sometimes akin to black magic,"
comments Griffin. "The techniques can be as
interesting as the effects of the illusion. And if
I show the techniques by illusory means, it
becomes all the more fun for me. While I was
not really a part of the art scene in the 1960's
and 1970's, there was a concept prevalent at

that time that exposing the materials of which an object is made could be as important as the object itself. Finally, the process becomes an autobiographical device, as I try to convey to the audience what was happening to me as I made the film or individual drawing.

"I've moved away from that in my more recent films," he continues. "I've become more concerned with content and story-telling. My films have tended to be humorous in a wry and rather cold way—I'd like to warm them up. I want to use more physical humor in my films, and explore the use of character animation, rather than doing something minimal and analytical."

Like many of his films, Griffin's publishing projects reflect his interest in the early days of animation. He speaks of Emile Cohl, Georges Melies, Oskar Fischinger, and the Fleischers as being among the artists who have influenced his work.

He adapted art from several of his films into flip books, and in 1980, he published a set of six flip books drawn by himself and five other independent animators through his Metropolis Graphics company.

When asked about the role of an independent animator, Griffin replies:

"The role of the independent animator? I'm not sure that isn't a contradiction in terms—that's asking what slot he fits in while he's saying he doesn't want a slot. One thing any independent filmmaker has to face is the problem of distribution. The advertising and promotional budgets for some studio features equal or exceed the amounts spent on the films themselves. An independent can make a film, but getting it before an audience is something quite different. Unless the artist is willing to examine that step, he'll never have a real niche, and he'll have to be sustained by grants and his parents.

"There's a danger in letting the marketplace determine what films you make," he cautions, "but it's balanced against the navel-gazing of a lot of independents who have no concern for who will see their films or how they will see them. The third alternative is the classic American dream, which is to be neither one nor the other, but a synthesis of the two."

FLYING FUR (1981): a loose, freewheeling piece in the genre of the Hollywood cartoon short.

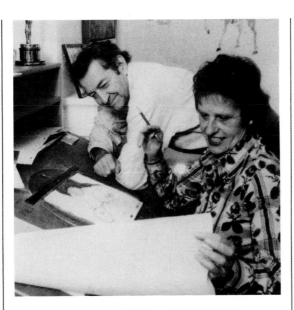

John Hubley (1914–1977) and Faith Hubley: The Animator's Animators

"I wouldn't do a film I didn't really believe in and love. I've reached the point where if I can't do exactly what I want to do in a film, I'd rather be a bartender."

—FAITH HUBLEY

For more than 20 years, Faith and the late John Hubley worked together creating some of the animated films most admired by other animators. Their efforts were rewarded with three Academy Awards (MOONBIRD, 1960; THE HOLE, 1963; and TIJUANA BRASS DOUBLE FEATURE, 1966), four more Oscar nominations (WINDY DAY, 1967; OF MEN AND DEMONS, 1969; VOYAGE TO NEXT, 1975; and A DOONESBURY SPECIAL, 1978), and dozens of awards from film festivals all over the world.

John Hubley studied to be a painter at Art Center in Los Angeles. Like many young artists, he was hired by the Disney studio during their talent searches in the mid-1930's. At Disney, Hubley painted backgrounds for SNOW WHITE and worked as an art director on PINOCCHIO, FANTASIA, DUMBO and BAMBI. He was an active participant in the Disney strike, and during the war he served in the animation division of the Air Force's Los Angeles Motion Picture Unit.

After the war, Hubley joined the newly founded UPA studio in a creative capacity. He is credited with being one of the major influences on that studio's boldly graphic style. In addition to designing the physical appearance of Mr. Magoo, he supervised and/or directed a number of the studio's cartoons, including ROOTY-TOOT-TOOT, arguably the studio's best film. In this highly stylized retelling of the saga of Frankie and Johnny, many of the elements that would later distinguish Hubley's personal films can already be seen: the linear figures, the exaggerated movements used to delineate the personalities of the characters, unconventional colors, and the use of multipass techniques.

Faith Elliot Hubley began her career in film as a script supervisor and film/music editor in Hollywood:

"I felt very isolated when I worked at the studios," she recalls; "It was like being stranded in a bottle at the bottom of the ocean. The people there just talked about the standard studio fare they were making. So when I was about 19, some friends and I organized a film society. Through its programs, I met cinema pioneer Georges Melies. From him I acquired a thirst to do noncommercial animation I've never lost. So my background was essentially in live-action; it wasn't until after I married Johnny that I began to work full time in animation."

She met John Hubley when she edited a sex education film, OF HUMAN GROWTH, which featured animation by UPA. The two became close friends and often discussed the need for other visions in animation. Faith soon returned to her native New York, and John remained in Los Angeles.

In 1952, John Hubley left UPA, largely due to the blacklisting of the McCarthy era. He set up his own studio, Storyboard, to do commercials. Not long afterward, he became involved in a proposed animated feature version of the musical FINIAN'S RAINBOW. Faith was also called in to assist John.

"I was sent out to sort of watch over Johnny," she explains. "He always worked at his own rhythm, and I had a reputation for always being on time and on budget. After the picture was shot down, I persuaded him to move to New York."

The Hubleys were married in 1955:

"Our marriage vows were to make one non-commercial film a year and to eat with the children we wanted to have."

The first major film they created together was ADVENTURES OF AN *, which the Guggenheim Museum commissioned in 1956. In it, the Hubleys sought to make animation even more graphic and stylized than it had been in the UPA films. Abstract and semiabstract characters were drawn in wax on paper and splashed with water colors "to produce a resisted texture." Imaginative use of abstraction, color, graphics, and multipass all became Hubley trademarks. These bold experiments, which were very influential on the work of European animators, suggested new directions for animation that were very different from the hard-outline cel techniques of the Hollywood studios.

At these studios, especially Disney, reality was carefully studied and caricatured to present a physical appearance of emotion and movement that would be recognizable on the screen. The Hubleys sought to present the same feelings and motions, but suggested them symbolically, using abstractions to depict what could not be shown in conventional pictorial terms. Instead of caricaturing the expressions and style of movement of someone in love, they used patterns of dots, lines, colors, and semiabstract figures to suggest the feelings of the couple in TENDER GAME (1958). Each approach represents a different way of seeing and rendering a subject. The Disney approach derives from the careful draftsmanship of the Renaissance masters; the Hubleys' method takes off from more contemporary artists like Matisse.

Faith Hubley's THE BIG BANG AND OTHER CREATION MYTHS (1981) combines modern scientific theories with various legends about the origins of the universe.

The title character from THE ADVENTURES OF AN * (1956), the first film on which John and Faith Hubley collaborated. The unusual texture was created by drawing the character in wax and splashing it with water colors.

MOONBIRD (1959): the Hubleys' Oscar-winning exploration of childhood fantasies.

For three of their best-known films—MOONBIRD (1959), WINDY DAY (1967), and COCKABOODY (1973)—the Hubleys recorded the voices of their children at play, edited the tapes and used the results as the sound track. The innovative results—a giggling, wandering story line—delighted some critics, who saw it as a profound treatment of childhood and development. Others disliked the films because they found them overly cute.

Many of the Hubley films deal with broader, less personal topics. OF STARS AND MEN (1962) probes man's relationship with the universe; THE HOLE (1963) discussed the possibilities of nuclear war. The striking EGGS (1970) is about overpopulation: A woman representing fertility carries on a dialogue with a man who symbolizes death to a jazzy score by Quincy Jones.

Fertility and Death discuss the future of the human race as they drive toward an unknown, unseen destination in EGGS (1970).

Zonker skin-diving in Walden Puddle provides a tranquil moment in A DOONESBURY SPECIAL (1977), the Hubleys' adaptation of Garry Trudeau's Pulitzer prize-winning comic strip.

The last project on which the Hubleys collaborated was A DOONESBURY SPECIAL (1977), a highly satisfying adaptation of Garry Trudeau's Pulitzer Prize-winning comic strip, that provides a wistful but humorous elegy to the 1960's and their idealism. John died during the storyboard stage.

Since then, Faith Hubley has maintained the studio, teaching, painting, and making films of her own: WHITHER WEATHER (1977), STEP BY STEP (1978), SKY DANCE (1979), and THE BIG BANG AND OTHER CREATION MYTHS (1981). She is currently completing ENTER LIFE for the Museum of Natural History/Smithsonian Institute, and has plans to animate a series of Native American sky myths.

"I still encounter some resistance to the idea of my being a woman involved in animation," she observes. "It's not a mean prejudice, but my situation is unexpected, and some people get uncomfortable. I've only found that true of older people; I've never encountered that attitude among younger people.

"I find it very encouraging that more women are getting involved in animation; I believe they're adding a special dimension. It strikes me as unhealthy to have all the practitioners of an art of the same sex. I'd feel the same way if almost all the animators were women."

After joking ruefully about the problems of distribution, she offers these thoughts about being an independent animator:

"An independent filmmaker should be active all the time. Once you decide what you want to say in a film, you can do storyboards or work out scenarios in your head for no money. But once you make a commitment to make a film, you should finish it. It may take time, raising the money may be hard, and the learning process may be difficult. But if your intentions are clear and you can see the film in your mind, how can you *not* finish it?"

A still from FRANK FILM, 1972.

Frank and Caroline Mouris: Animation and Collage

"You either end up with a nervous breakdown or a viable film."

—FRANK MOURIS

When Frank Mouris won the Oscar for animated short in 1973 for his dazzling FRANK FILM, observers asked what previous experience in film this obviously talented young animator had. The answer was none. Except for two rolls of tests, Mouris and his wife, Caroline, had never made a film before. (Although the award was given to Frank, he and Caroline work as a creative team on all their projects, a fact he is quick to point out.)

"I got into animation by luck," says Mouris, his words punctuated by his easy laugh. "I studied architecture in college, but I didn't like it because it was something one person couldn't do. I switched to graphic design in graduate school at Yale; that was something one person could do, but I didn't enjoy it. The chairman of my committee suggested I try animation. As I don't like to draw, I used cutouts—I had been making collages of them

for years. I shot one test reel on a jerry-built animation stand they had in the chemistry department: That and one other reel of tests were the only things I had filmed before I made FRANK FILM."

Mouris explains that FRANK FILM grew out of his lifelong obsession with magazines. He saved mountains of them, until the problem of storage space reached crisis proportions. He took to cutting out the pages with images that interested him, but these, too, soon grew too numerous to store. So he began to cut out just the images he wanted and sorted them into boxes. He started using these images to make collages. (Apparently, his fascination with magazines continues: During the course of this interview, Mouris casually mentioned he had nine grocery bags of magazines he had "processed" waiting to be taken to the local dump.)

FRANK FILM can be seen as the ultimate collage. Every frame overflows with images cut from countless magazines. Dozens of cats from cat food ads move by means of photokinesis. Hundreds of fingers that displayed nail polish colors form kaleidoscopic patterns. Thousands of eyes stare back at the audience. The sound track, created by Tony Schwartz, combines an autobiographical narrative with a sonic collage of words beginning with the letter "F." The result is almost overwhelming: The viewer is immersed in visual and vocal imagery. The film functions both as Mouris's autobiography and a commentary on society's consumerism.

Since FRANK FILM, the Mourises have created several other films that combine live-action footage with single-frame techniques and some animation. CONEY ISLAND is a documentary about the famous amusement park; SCREENTEST deals with a group of New York eccentrics. AND THEN . . . , a dramatic short, made with a grant from the American Film Institute, features live-action segments, slow motion, speeded-up action, and still photographs.

"We try to bring the every-frame-counts attitude of animation to our live-action work," Mouris comments. "Animation has helped us a lot: It's made us extremely good editors. We're used to looking at individual frames and not wasting any screen time, not holding any image on the screen longer than necessary for it to achieve its maximum impact.

"Animation also taught us that the camera can be *anywhere.* There's no reason for a live-action film to be just a filmed stage play. In a film, the camera can be shifted anywhere and the actors can do anything. The most exciting filmmaking occurs when you create magic."

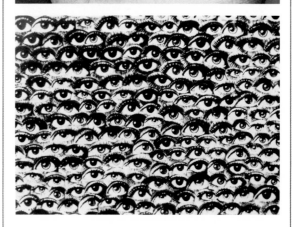

Stills from FRANK FILM (1972): thousands of images that had been cut from magazines were pasted on cels then assembled in layers to produce these visuals.

Currently, the Mourises are at work on a script for a live-action feature. They are also planning an animated sequel to FRANK FILM, this one about Caroline. Its title: FRANKLY CAROLINE. ("She's quite outspoken," observes Mouris.)

Another Mouris collage demonstrates the juxtaposition of images found in their work.

ART ON PAGES 107-109 © FRANK MOURIS

"We're trying to make this one less hard-edged and more abstract—messy, punky, funky, and painterly—more like the abstract expressionist painting we both enjoy," explains Mouris. "The images for FRANK FILM were all pasted on cels; we have a suspicion that FRANKLY CAROLINE may all be done on paper. We're using multiple images again, but not stacks of images on cels. We're sort of backing into the film with a vague idea of what we want. We hope to discover how to achieve it on film: We discovered the stacking method of FRANK FILM while we were working under the camera."

When he turns to the question of the role of the independent filmmaker, Mouris grows almost serious and offers these thoughts to aspiring artists:

"Animation and single-frame techniques are still the cheapest ways to begin making films, because they're so labor intensive. You can do it all yourself and be everything—director, producer, sound, editor, etc—which makes it excellent preparation for later, more challenging films.

"The limitations of inexpensive equipment can also help you in the beginning," he adds. "If you have only 100 sheets of paper and a camera with very limited capabilities, it's what you'll put into the artwork on those 100 pages that will be important: It will have to be.

"Finally, it never hurts to have something you can do to earn the money to support your filmmaking habit. In the beginning, it's nice not to have to support the habit with commercial films that might taint your personal ones, although there are people who manage to juggle the two. I did graphic work for a while."

His thoughtful demeanor crumbles and the more characteristic humor returns as he segues from the general problems of the independent to his own experience:

"Independent filmmakers provide the only way new things get done in film. Studio techniques evolve along certain lines—they have to. But independents have nothing to lose, they're completely free to do what they want. We *knew* no one would care about an autobiographical animated film, so we made it to please ourselves, to get it out of our systems, so we could get on with making commercial films. Success ruined that whole plan—now we're seeing how long we can get away with doing what we want."

Lotte Reiniger (1899–1981): The Animator as Shadow Artist

For most of its 75-year history, animation has been an almost exclusively male domain. In the early days of the medium, most animators came from the ranks of aspiring or professional newspaper cartoonists and magazine illustrators, traditionally male occupations in the earlier part of this century. One major exception to this rule was Lotte Reiniger, who pioneered the technique of making shadow or silhouette films.

Born in Berlin in 1899, Reiniger recalled that she could "cut a silhouette almost a soon as I could manage to hold a pair of scissors." As a child, she created shadow plays, which allowed her to express her love of the threatre within the small confines of her parents' apartment and gave her the opportunity to develop her skills at cutting paper forms.

Reiniger's first experience with animation came in 1918, when she worked for Paul Wegener on a film version of THE PIED PIPER OF HAMLIN. When neither live rats nor guinea pigs could be made to cooperate with the demands of the script, Reiniger and a number of her co-workers moved wooden rats in stop-motion animation. The film, for which she also did elaborate cut-paper titles, was a great success. In her later writings, she always spoke of this initiation into the process of animation with great affection and warmth.

In 1919, she created her first silhouette film, THE ORNAMENT OF THE LOVESTRUCK HEART. Reiniger made her cutouts from heavy paper and thin sheets of lead. She manipulated them under the camera (using the method described in Chapter 2) to create the illusion of motion. Her sensitivity to styles of movement enabled her to create vivid characters with her paper figures. Her artistry with scissors was extraordinary, and her figures and settings are marked by a delicacy and an intricacy that are immediately recognizable.

In her films, Reiniger combined both the traditions of the paper cut and the shadow puppet. The paper cut is a traditional folk art in Eastern Europe and China: Peasant women cut decorations for their homes out of colored paper. (Chinese paper cuts, many of them quite intricate, are still sold in stores specializing in imports and oriental art.) The shadow puppet theatre has a long history in India, the Middle East, China, and Java. Puppets made of delicately cut animal hide are held against a translucent screen and illuminated from behind. From the later 18th century through World War I, shadow theatres were very popular in Europe. Reiniger's films can be seen as a bridge linking these traditional arts with the 20th century invention of film.

After making several films based on such familiar fairy tales as SLEEPING BEAUTY and CINDERELLA, Reiniger turned her attention to a highly ambitious project in 1923: a feature-length film entitled THE ADVENTURES OF PRINCE ACHMED. Working with her husband, filmmaker Carl Koch, and two assistants (plus

Reiniger at work on PRINCE ACHMED in Potsdam, near Berlin, 1924. She preferred to work kneeling, bent over the surface on which she manipulated the figures.

Stills from PRINCE ACHMED illustrate the filagreed delicacy and shadow effect Reiniger could achieve with a pair of scissors.

occasional help from animator Berthold Bartosch), she completed PRINCE ACHMED in 3 years. Although it was not the first animated feature, as is sometimes claimed, it is one of the earliest features that is still shown. PRINCE ACHMED is a handsome film that contains a number of striking effects, created by moving paper waves and stars on various levels at different speeds under the camera—a technique that anticipated the multiplane camera.

Reiniger at work at the National Film Board of Canada studio in 1975, more than fifty years after PRINCE ACHMED.

COURTESY OF THE NATIONAL FILM BOARD OF CANADA

Reiniger's version of the fairy tale AUCASSIN AND NICOLETTE (1975): pieces of colored tissue paper were placed within the dark, silhouette framework to produce the brightly-colored highlights.

COURTESY OF THE NATIONAL FILM BOARD OF CANADA

Despite the popularity of PRINCE ACHMED, Reiniger never made another feature. After its completion, she made a number of short films on various subjects: themes from operas, like PAPAGENO (1935), fairy tales like Hans Christian Andersen's THE CHINESE NIGHTIN-GALE (1927), and the Dr. Doolittle stories of Hugh Lofting. In 1936, she moved to England where she continued her work with films like DAUGHTER (1937), that featured music by Benjamin Britten. In 1937, she also created a Chinese shadow theatre for Jean Renoir's LA MARSEILLAISE; Carl Koch collaborated on the film as scenarist.

After spending several years in Italy and Germany, Reiniger returned to England in 1949 where she directed a number of films, some of them remakes of her older films, for television. Several of these later versions had translucent colors added to the black-and-white of the silhouettes, an effect created with colored tissue paper.

In her later years, Reiniger gave lectures and workshops throughout North America and Western Europe on shadow animation and her own techniques. In 1975, she made AUCASSIN AND NICOLETTE at the National Film Board of Canada. Her last film, THE ROSE AND THE RING, was completed in 1979 during her stay in Canada. Lotte Reiniger died in 1981 in Dettenhausen, West Germany, at the age of 82.

Although Reiniger generously shared her methods in her lectures and in her book *Shadow Puppets, Shadow Theatres and Shadow Films,* no one has surpassed or even equaled her skill and artistry in this special-ized area of animation. Her talent and dedica-tion to her art make Lotte Reiniger an inspirational figure to all aspiring animators.

International animation is a curious entity, at once fragmented and united, cosmopolitan and parochial. As with all the visual arts, regional styles and schools can be identified, although the artists who establish those styles may come from disparate backgrounds. Animators often live and work in several countries during the course of their careers. For example, Julius Pinschewer, the father of Swiss animation, was born in Posen in what was then Prussia (now Poznań, Poland), and exhibited his first films in Berlin.

One reason for this pattern of movement is the perennial shortage of funding for animated films: animators tend to go where work and financing are available. Animator Paul Driessen has made films in England and Canada, as well as his native Holland. Artistic and political freedom may also be consider-ations: the two most prominent Polish animators, Jan Lenica and Walerian Borowczyk, left Poland in the 1950's.

The potential of animation to transcend linguistic, cultural, and political boundaries is hampered by limited and often erratic distribution. For example, British commercials are seen on television and in theatres in Europe, Africa, and the Middle East, but rarely in the United States or South America. Disney features are released all over the world, and THE FLINTSTONES enjoys large audiences on Eastern European television. But few European films are shown in the United States. As a rule, animated films are produced for a specific, usually domestic market, with international distribution—when it can be obtained—providing supplemental income.

Little has been written about world animation, and only a small part of what has been written is reliable. No biographies exist of significant figures such as Julius Pinschewer, Len Lye, or Alexander Alexeieff. Histories and commentaries about animation in a specific country are usually written with a domestic audience in mind. Few books on animation are translated into other languages or made available in other countries.

To list all the animation studios and animators in the world would require a volume larger than this one. Such a list would also require constant updating, as individuals enter the animation industry or retire from it, and as companies form, disband, and merge. This chapter examines some of the major producers of animated films in various parts of the world, but it is by no means complete. Readers curious to know more about frame-by-frame filmmaking in a specific country should contact the consulate of that country for further information.

EASTERN EUROPE

In the years since World War II, Eastern Europe has come to be recognized as a source of artistically significant animated films. Production there tends to be centered around government-sponsored studios, with about half of each year's production directed toward children. However, these animators earn their reputations for their "adult" films.

Some Eastern European films are funny: Ferenc Rofusz's Oscar-winning short THE FLY (1980), produced at Pannonia Film Studios in Hungary, is an extremely clever gag film. But Eastern European animation is more typically characterized by a dark gallows humor that centers on alienation and frustration, like Marcell Jankovic's elegant, calligraphic retelling of the legend of *Sisyphus*.

The horrors of the Nazi occupation and the subsequent political domination by the Soviet Union are reflected in many Eastern European animated films. The political implications of a work like Katja Georgi's THE RIVER, produced at DEFA Studio in East Germany, offer a case in point. A young man and woman are separated by a river that grows wider as they try to find a place to cross it. Eventually the tiny figures and broad stream are lost in the grey landscape. The image of the frustrated lovers, separated by a barrier they cannot bridge, is a haunting one; the obvious depth of feeling with which it is presented leaves the viewer with a lasting impression.

Poland

It is significant that the two most respected Polish animators have chosen to work in France and West Germany. Jan Lenica began his career as a poster artist. He turned to animation only after leaving Poland. His films are filled with black, often nightmarish imagery. In LABYRINTH (1961), a man is captured. His head is drilled open, a funnel is inserted and a fluid is poured in. The opening is sealed and the man is set free. The central character in A (1964) is haunted by a gigantic letter "A." After being driven nearly insane, he manages to destroy the "A"—only to have an equally huge "B" appear in its place.

Walerian Borowczyk enjoys an even greater reputation. Some observers consider him one of the most artistically significant animators of the postwar era. His most striking work is LE JEU DES ANGES (GAME OF ANGELS) (1964), a chilling evocation of the horrors of the Nazi extermination camps. The film is a collage of images—moving trains, stark walls and cells, pipes and dark flowing liquids—punctuated by the falling wings of the sorrowing angels. No violence is depicted—indeed, the only human seen is a booted female prisoner with a shaven head—but the subject of the film is disturbingly clear.

A number of well-respected animators continue to work in Poland, including Witold Giersz, Jerzy Zitzman, Miroslaw Kijowicz, and Daniel Szczechura. The country's principal studios include Miniatur, Se-Ma-Four, and Cracow Short Film.

Czechoslovakia

The most celebrated animator in Czech filmmaking is the master of puppet animation, Jiri Trnka (1912–1969). Trnka ran a puppet theatre from 1935 to 1938 and, after the war, he founded the animation unit of the nationalized Czech cinema. He began by doing cel

SISYPHUS by Marcell Jankovics (Hungary): an understated, graphic parable of human frustration.

THE RIVER (East Germany): Katja Georgi's poignant study of two lovers separated by an insurmountable boundary.

COURTESY OF PHOENIX FILMS AND VIDEO, INC. PHOTO DEFA/POHLER

animation, at which he achieved a limited success. However, one of his drawn films enjoyed considerable popularity: THE DEVIL ON SPRINGS, also known as THE CHIMNEY SWEEP (1946), a savagely anti-Nazi short.

In 1947, he produced his first puppet film, THE CZECH YEAR, which he followed with a version of Hans Christian Andersen's THE EMPEROR'S NIGHTINGALE in 1947. In 1955, he completed a feature-length puppet film of A MIDSUMMER NIGHT'S DREAM, which some Shakespearean scholars consider the most successful cinematic adaptation of the play. Perhaps his most poignant film is his last: THE HAND (1965). A monstrous human hand forces a tiny sculptor to create a portrait of it, over the artist's objections. The melancholy with which Trnka imbues the figure of the sculptor is both moving and eloquent.

A number of other animators have followed Trnka's work and the long tradition of central European puppet theatres to create excellent puppet films. Those artists include Bretislav Pojar, Jan Svankmajer, Hermina Tyrlova, and Karl Zeman, who also enjoys a distinguished career as a live-action director. In addition, numerous drawn animation films have been produced in Czechoslovakia.

Bulgaria

Although there were attempts at making animated films at the Sofia Studio as early as 1949, Bulgarian animation is usually considered to have begun in 1955 with the completion of MARKO THE HERO by Todor Dinov of that studio. Trained in Moscow by Russian animators, Dinov remained an important force in Bulgarian animation throughout the 1960's; his best known works are THE LIGHTNING ROD (1962) and THE DAISY (1965).

Working in a very simple, yet charming style, Donyo Donev brought whimsy to Bulgarian films in the early 1970's with works like THE THREE FOOLS, DECEMBER, THE INTELLIGENT VILLAGE, and DE FACTO. The latter is a droll little story in which each worker attempts to prove that it wasn't his fault their recently constructed building collapsed. (The blame is finally fixed on the music of a nearby spectator's flute.)

Currently, the Sofia Studio produces about twenty films each year. The recently established Varna Animation Festival promises to bring Bulgaria a more prominent place in world animation.

East Germany

When the Council of Ministers founded the VEB DEFA Studio for Trickfilms in 1955, animators had already been working in the country for at least 5 years. Located in Dresden, the studio currently has a staff of about 250. To date, DEFA has produced more than 850 short films for television and theatrical release. Drawn, puppet, and silhouette techniques have been used to create entertainment films and documentaries. Among the best known artists at DEFA are Bruno Böttge, Günter Rätz, Kurt Weiler, Otto Sacher, and Klaus and Katja Georgi. In 1982, Rätz produced the country's first animated feature, a puppet film entitled THE FLYING WINDMILL.

Yugoslavia

To animate: to give life and soul to a design, not through the copying but through the transformation of reality.
—COLLECTIVE STATEMENT BY THE ANIMATORS OF ZAGREB FILM

Yugoslavian animation is centered almost exclusively around the justly celebrated Zagreb Studio, one of the three branches of Zagreb Film. When the animation unit was established in 1954, many of the artists who came to work there were veterans of the ill-fated Duga Film that Fadil Hadzic had founded 5 years earlier.

While the policy of Duga Film had been to emulate the full animation of the Disney studio, the artists at Zagreb Film were inspired by the work of UPA, particularly Bob Cannon's GERALD MCBOING-BOING and John Hubley's animated inserts for the live-action film THE FOUR POSTER. (The work of Zagreb Film bears more affinities to American animation than that of any other Eastern European studio.) Most of these artists had little, if any, training in animation. Some had been newspaper cartoonists, but others came from such diverse backgrounds as law, architecture, and journalism.

The output of the Zagreb Studio for its first 2 years was devoted to advertising films, but in 1956 they produced their first story film, THE PLAYFUL ROBOT, which was screened at several festivals. World attention really came to Zagreb in 1958 when OPENING NIGHT by Nikola Kostelac and Vjekoslav Kostanjsek was screened at the Cannes Festival. As the work of UPA declined in the late 1950's and early 1960's, Zagreb came to be recognized as *the* center of aesthetic experimentation and innovation in animation.

DIE PRINZESSIN UND DER ZIEGENHIRT (THE PRINCESS AND THE GOATHERD) from DEFA Studios (East Germany).

DAS GLUCK DES FALKNERS (THE LUCK OF THE FALKNERS) from DEFA Studios (East Germany).

The Zagreb Studio has always maintained a highly collaborative structure with individuals changing roles from film to film. The director of one film may work as the designer for another and write the script for a third. However, it is possible to point out the work of specific artists.

Dusan Vukotic is generally regarded as the guiding spirit of the studio. He directed THE PLAYFUL ROBOT, and satirized American westerns and gangster films in COWBOY JIMMY (1957) and CONCERTO FOR SUB-MACHINE GUN (1959). In 1961, he created ERSATZ, about a brightly colored world of inflatable toys, drawn in a style derived from Kandinsky and Klee. ERSATZ became the first foreign film to win the Academy Award for animated short.

The animators of Zagreb worked in a variety of styles and moods. Pavao Statler and Branko Ranitovoc evoked the world of Edgar Allan Poe in their brooding retelling of THE MASQUE OF THE RED DEATH. Zlatko Grgic delighted audiences with the macabre wit of THE MUSICAL PIG in 1965. He created the character of Professor Balthasar, the star of a popular series of children's films, that same year in INVENTOR OF SHOES. Borivoj Dovnikovic displayed an outre sense of humor in films like THE FLOWER LOVERS (1970), in which blossoms explode in the delighted faces of anyone who sniffs them, and ZZ (1977), a film about a little man who can't find a badly needed bathroom. Other well-known animators at Zagreb include Vatroslav Mimica, Aleksander Marks, Boris Kolar, Zlatko Bourek, Vlado Kristl, Nedeljko Dragic, and Milan Blazekovic.

Zagreb Film continues to produce about 4 hours of animation each year. Although the studio lost its preeminent place to the National Film Board of Canada during the 1970's, it still remains one of the most widely respected centers of creativity in animation. Zagreb has also been the site of one of the world's major animation festivals since 1972.

Hungary

While written evidence suggests that experimentation with animation and other forms of filmmaking may have begun in Hungary as early as 1896, no filmic records survive. Indeed, little remains of any films made there before the end of World War II.

Marcell Jankovics' THE WHITE MARE'S SON (Hungary) is an opulent visual tapestry: some observers consider it the most visually innovative feature since YELLOW SUBMARINE.

COURTESY OF HUNGAROFILM/BUDAPEST

In 1956, a group of trained artists who had been working at the fledgling Hungarian Film Productions Company founded the Pannonia Film Studio. By the end of the decade, several artists at Pannonia had received international recognition for their animated films, including Gyula Mackassy and György Varnai for PENCIL AND INDIA RUBBER and DUEL, and Tibor Csermak for THE BALL WITH WHITE DOTS.

During the 1960's, most of the output of Pannonia was devoted to short films for television, many of them based on stories from Hungarian history or national folk tales. Hungarian animated films received increasing critical recognition and won prizes at major festivals during the 1970's: MODERN SPORTS COACHING (1970) by Bela Ternovsky, SISYPHUS (1974) and FIGHT (1977) by Marcell Jankovics, SCENES WITH BEANS (1975) by Otto Foky, and THE FLY (1980) by Ferenc Rofusz.

In 1973, Jankovics completed the first Hungarian animated feature, JANOS VITEZ (variously translated as VALIANT JOHN, JOHN THE HERO and JOHNNY CORNCOB) for the celebrations of the 150th birthday of the poet-revolutionary Sandor Petöfi. Jankovics' most recent film, THE WHITE MARE'S SON (1981) is considered by some critics to be the most visually innovative feature since YELLOW SUBMARINE.

Soviet Union

The first Soviet animated films served the same purpose as political posters: the transmission of messages simply and clearly to large numbers of people, many of whom were illiterate. Short satirical cartoon sequences were incorporated by Dziga Vertov into his live-action film magazine *Cine-Truth* in 1922. Under the supervision of Vértov, A. Bushkin and Alexander Ivanov created the first animated film in the Soviet Union in 1924: SOVIET TOYS. All these early films carried propaganda messages. The best known of them is CHINA IN FLAMES (1925), by N. Khodataev, Y. Merkulov, and Z. Komissarenko, which depicted the enslavement of the Chinese peasantry by Imperialistic forces.

Two years later, the first children's animated film was created: SENKA, THE AFRICAN (1927), directed by Ivan Ivanov-Vano, who subsequently became one of the country's most prolific animation directors.

The screening of several Disney shorts at the First International Film Festival in Moscow in 1935 greatly influenced Soviet animators. The Disney films generated an increased interest in drawn animation in a country where cutouts had been the standard medium. The organization of the Disney Studio, with its division of labor and crew system, was used as a model when the Soyuzmultfilm Studio was established the following year.

The first Soviet animated feature was completed in 1935, a puppet/live action combination entitled THE NEW GULLIVER by Alexander Ptuschko, who introduced a proletarian revolution into Swift's Lilliputia. Four years later, he produced another live action puppet feature, THE LITTLE GOLDEN KEY, based on a popular Russian story.

A variety of styles are apparent in the animated films from the USSR: (right, clockwise from top) MUSICIANS FROM BREMEN, (bottom, right) UNDER AND OVER! (bottom, left) MITTEN, (center left) MAGIC RING. (Opposite page) TIGER CUB ON A SUNFLOWER.

(Clockwise from top left) MERRY-GO-ROUND, THE ADVENTURES OF SOLNYSHKIN, MOROZ IVANOVICH, A REVENGE MATCH, GIRAFFE AND EYE-GLASSES, THE HERITAGE OF MAGICIAN BAKHRAM, **and** IF YOU DON'T LIKE IT, DO NOT LISTEN.

COURTESY OF SOVEXPORT FILM, USSR

During World War II, Soviet animators were either drafted or removed to Samarkand, where they made propaganda and training films. Following the war, a number of animated features were produced, many of them based on folk tales: THE LITTLE HUNCHBACKED HORSE (1948), THE LITTLE SNOW MAIDEN (1952), THE TWELVE MONTHS (1956), and THE MECHANICAL FLEA (1964) by Ivanov-Vano; CRIMSON FLOWER (1952), THE GOLDEN ANTELOPE (1954), and THE SNOW QUEEN (1957) by L. Atamanov; THE BEWITCHED BOY (1955) by V. Polkovnikov and A. Snezhko-Blotzkaya; and ADVENTURES OF BURATINO (1960) by D. Babichenko and Ivanov-Vano.

The "modern" period of Soviet animation is considered to have begun in 1962 with a series of films by new artists: THE STORY OF ONE CRIME by F. Khitruk, THE BATH by S. Yutkevitch and A. Karanovitch, BIG TROUBLE by V. and Z. Brumberg, and WHO SAID "MEOW"? by V. Degatyarev. During the later 1960's, directors N. Serebryakov and V. Kurchevsky came to prominence with films like I AM WAITING FOR A NESTLING (1966), THE TRAIN OF MEMORY (1975), and THE SEPARATED ONE (1981) by Serebryakov, and THE LEGEND OF GRIEG (1967) and RICH SADKO (1975) by Kurchevsky.

The 1970's also saw the establishment of animation studios in some of the other Soviet Republics. Artists like E. Turganov and R. Raamat in Estonia, A. Burovs in Latvia, and I. Gurvich and D. Cherkassky in the Ukraine have gained international recognition for their work. Within the last few years, a number of younger animators in the USSR have attracted attention, too, including A. Petrov, G. Sokolov, Y. Norshtein, and I. Garanina. The Soviet animation industry continues to produce about 100 films each year.

WESTERN EUROPE

Animation has been a part of Western European culture since the inception of the art form. Animators in this region have worked with so many styles and subjects that diversity is the only quality the films of the artists in the various countries share.

West Germany

Although some experimental animation was done in Germany prior to World War I, it was only after the war that the art form came into its own there. The Weimar era produced an impressive array of abstract and experimental short films by artists interested in expanding the potential of the medium. Animation was considered an art form, and many of these films parallel developments that were occurring in the other visual arts in Germany at that time.

In 1921, Walter Ruttman premiered his painted-on-glass film, LIGHTPLAY, OPUS 1, in Frankfurt. Hans Richter and Swedish-born Viking Eggeling collaborated on a number of experimental shorts between 1919 and 1925. At about the same time, Oskar Fischinger was conducting his wax-slicing experiments (see Chapter 5), which he followed with his attempts to create visual music in his STUDIES series during the early 1930's. Lotte Reiniger made her first silhouette film, THE ORNAMENT OF THE LOVESTRUCK HEART, in 1919, and in 1926, she completed THE ADVENTURES OF PRINCE ACHMED, one of the first feature-length animated films.

This rich era of experimentation ended with the rise of the Nazi regime, for which all nonrepresentational art was anathema. Some animated films were made during World War II in the Fascist and occupied countries of Europe, but few of them have survived.

The diverse graphic styles of Hans Bacher's SHERLOCK HOLMES (left) and John Coates DER SCHNEEMANN, "The Snowman" from the Fishereosen Studio (right) attest to the vitality of animation in West Germany.

"After the war," comments animator Hans Bacher, "the German people had to rebuild their country—they had no interest in animation. The children loved the Disney films, but once they grew up, they were expected to work and be serious. There were no schools or classes; no one who could or would teach animation. That situation began to change in the 1970's: Animation classes were offered at the universities, but they were primitive at best—all the equipment was handmade."

Today, there are about two dozen animation studios in West Germany, with an additional 50 or so free-lance animators at work. Most German animation is used for educational films, commercials, and titles. Some short films have been made by artists like Helmut Herbst and Wolfgang Urchs. Like the Eastern European shorts, these films tend to reflect the destruction and division of the country produced by the war.

Belgium

Although animated films were first used in Belgium as early as 1922 to train recruits in the armed forces, little exploration of the medium occurred there until after World War II. Claude Misonne produced the first Belgian animated feature in 1948, a puppet film entitled THE CRAB WITH THE GOLDEN CLAWS. The film exerted little influence, and the few animated films produced in Belgium during the next decade were derived from Disney.

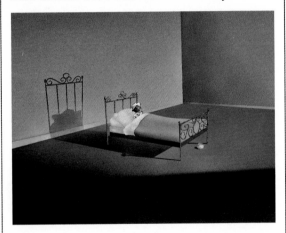

In 1960, Raoul Servais created his first film HARBOUR LIGHTS. He quickly rose to prominence as the most respected animator in Belgium, and has won numerous awards for his ten short films. His most recent work, HARPYA, a dark story about a man haunted by a hideous harpy, won the grand prize for short films at Cannes in 1979.

The Belgian government has assisted the animation industry with grants and free loans: more than 18 studios now exist in Belgium, most of them specializing in short films and commercials. Since the late 1960's, a number of joint Franco-Belgian features have been produced, based on the adventures of popular European comic-strip characters, including Lucky Luke, Tintin, the Schtroumpfs (known in America as the Smurfs), and Asterix the Gaul.

France

The early years of French animation were dominated by Emile Cohl, who produced approximately 300 short films in America and France between 1908 and 1923. Financially ruined by the war, the destitute and forgotten Cohl retired to a home for the aged, where he remained until his death in 1938. Since then, French animation has largely been dominated by artists from other countries. The two most famous animated films made in France, L'IDÉE (THE IDEA) and UNE NUIT SUR LE MONT CHAUVE (NIGHT ON BALD MOUNTAIN), were made by foreigners.

THE IDEA (1932) was created by the Czech animator and painter Berthold Bartosch. Based on a series of woodcuts by Frans Masereel, the film uses a number of techniques—cutouts, collages, and drawings—to tell an allegory of an artist's idea that leads the workers in their struggle against the State, Church, etc. The film caused a scandal in its day, and was quickly banned. NIGHT ON BALD MOUNTAIN (1933) was the first film created by the late Alexander Alexeieff and Claire Parker on their newly-invented pinscreen. An eerie, metamorphic evocation of Mussorgsky's music, the film remains as powerful today as it was nearly 50 years ago.

Several other foreign animators have produced important films in France, including Lenica and Borowczyk. The American artist Hector Hopkins and the English illustrator Anthony Gross animated the pastorale JOIE DE VIVRE in 1934, and INDIAN RHAPSODY, a segment of a projected feature based on Jules

HARPYA: Raoul Servais' chilling story about a terrible mythological monster.

Verne's AROUND THE WORLD IN 80 DAYS, in 1953. The Russian puppet animator Ladislas Starevitch produced several films in France, among them the exquisitely detailed ROMAN DE RENARD (THE STORY OF THE FOX) in 1938.

Currently, the most respected native French animator is Paul Grimault, who founded the studio Les Gemeaux with Andre Sarrut during the 1930's. Production on their first feature, GO CHEZ LES OISEAUX, was halted in 1939 by the outbreak of the war; the film was completed in 1943 under the title LES PASSAGÉRES DE LA GRANDE OURSE (THE PASSENGERS OF THE BIG DIPPER). Grimault remained active during the war, when the absence of American films in France gave him easier access to audiences.

In 1947, Grimault and writer-poet Jacques Prevert began work on an adaptation of a story by Hans Christian Andersen, LA BERGERE ET LE RAMONEUR (THE SHEPHERDESS AND THE CHIMNEY-SWEEP); the production was plagued with problems, and both partners disowned the finished film. In 1967, they reacquired the rights and reworked the film, changing the title to LE ROI ET L'OISEAU (THE KING AND THE BIRD).

Animation remains a vital art form in France; many animators continue to make commercials and short films. And although Rene Laloux and Roland Topor enjoy a certain cult following for their feature LA PLANETE SAUVAGE (SAVAGE PLANET) (1972), none of the younger animators enjoys an international reputation comparable to that of Grimault or Alexeieff.

Italy

Some experimentation with animation took place in Italy between 1916 and 1924, but little attention was paid to the medium until 1940, when several production companies were formed. Among the films produced at this time were Gino Parenti's BRAVO ANSELMO and an hour-long, black-and-white version of PINOCCHIO by Cartoni Animati Italiani. Plans were made to redo the latter film in color, but were never realized. Indeed, at least a half dozen animated features have been started in Italy and never completed, including a biography of Mussolini that Guido Pregepi began in 1923.

During two periods of productivity, the later 1940's and the 1960's, a number of short films and features, including Pino Zac's FILIPO THE CAT (1965) and THE NON EXISTENT KNIGHT (1969) were made by Italian animators, but they found very limited audiences outside of Italy.

The best-known Italian animator is the Milanese Bruno Bozzetto, who made his debut in 1958 with TAPUM, THE HISTORY OF WEAPONS. Two years later, he created his most popular character, the Italian Everyman, Mr. Rossi in AN OSCAR FOR MR. ROSSI; the character proved so popular that Bozzetto used him in numerous other shorts. But despite the popularity of his short films, Bozzetto's international reputation rests primarily on ALLEGRO NON TROPPO (1976), a collection of animated sequences set to classical music that spoofs Disney's

Life emerges from the contents of a Coke bottle and embarks on a delightfully skewed story of evolution in the "Bolero" sequence of Bruno Bozzetto's ALLEGRO NON TROPPO (Italy).

FANTASIA. The more memorable sequences include a wistful portrait of an abandoned house cat (Sibelius' Valse Triste), a madcap protest against conformity and militarism (Dvorak's Slavonic Dance No. 7), and a delightfully skewed history of evolution (Ravel's Bolero).

Other animators continue to work in Italy, either as independents, like Guilio Gianini and Emmanuele Luzzati, or in studios like Cineteam Realizzazione in Rome. To date, the Italian contribution to animation has been surprisingly small, especially when contrasted with the significance of the work done by live-action Italian filmmakers.

England

Although artists like Arthur Melbourne-Cooper, Harry Furniss, and Walter Booth experimented with animation before World War I, and a few studios were established in the 1920's—the best known being the G. F. Studdy studio who created the dog, Bonzo—American films dominated the theatres. British animation did not come into its own until after World War II.

Len Lye and Norman McLaren did significant

experimental animation in England during the 1930's. Lye completed the first drawn-on-film project, COLOR BOX, in 1935; McLaren did the first of what would be many drawn-on-film shorts in 1938: LOVE ON THE WING. These films also had to contain public service messages because they were sponsored by the General Post Office. During the war, British animation was channeled into propaganda and training films.

Perhaps the most remarkable thing about postwar British animation is its vitality and diversity. No trace of bitterness over the dissolution of the overseas empire or the status of England in the postwar world is evident in their animated films. About 70 studios exist in Britain; most of them produce commercials for Europe, Africa, and the Middle East. The level of quality is generally high.

The oldest animation studio in England is Halas & Batchelor, founded by the husband and wife team of John Halas and Joy Batchelor in 1940. In a little over 40 years, the studio has produced over 2,000 short films and four features. Among the latter are the first British full-length animated film, HANDLING SHIPS, an instructional work still in use in some parts of the world, and the first entertainment feature, an adaptation of George Orwell's ANIMAL FARM (1954). The Halas-Batchelor studio was also a leader in the development of animated educational films and commercials in London. In addition, John Halas has written several books on the subject, including *Visual Scripting* and, with Roger Manvell, *Art in Movement* and *The Techniques of Film Animation.*

Richard Williams Animation has become one of the major influences in British animation, winning an Oscar in 1972 for their adaptation of Dickens' A CHRISTMAS CAROL. The Williams

WIRE MAGI by RAI-TV & Cineteam Realizzazione, Italy.

Four strikingly different styles of animation from Richard Williams (London, Hollywood): (right) A stylized cossack gallops past the engine of the Trans-Siberian Railway for Count Pushkin Vodka; (center) a Frazetta-inspired warrior for Jovan Musk Oil; (far right) a realistic panther for UniRoyal Tires in Australia; (lower right) a rock 'n' roll bear for Cresca Soda.

studio has produced some commercials that are brilliantly animated, including a spot for Jovan Musk Oil, in the style of fantasy illustrator Frank Frazetta, a wildly rocking bear for Cresca soda, a semiabstract evocation of Imperial Russia for Count Pushkin Vodka, and the title sequences for THE RETURN OF THE PINK PANTHER and THE PINK PANTHER STRIKES AGAIN. For more than a decade, Williams' animators have been working part-time on a feature, THE THIEF.

TV Cartoons Ltd., usually referred to as TVC, produced the BEATLES series (1965–68) and THE LION, THE WITCH, AND THE WARDROBE (1979) for American television in conjunction with Bill Melendez Productions. In 1967, the artists at TVC created the feature YELLOW SUBMARINE, a brilliant but flawed film that marked a turning point in the history of animation. More recently, the studio did two sequences for HEAVY METAL (1981).

Other highly respected studios are Bob Godfrey Films, Wyatt-Cattaneo, The Producers, Ian Moo Young, and Grand Slamm Animation. Many British animators use their commercial work to finance their personal films. Geoff Dunbar of Grand Slamm brought the style and imagery of Toulouse Lautrec to life in LAUTREC (1975), and captured the brutality of Alfred Jarrey's *Ubu Roi* in his film UBU. Oscar Grillo of The Producers, who has done fine animation of loose-limbed, embracing animals for a Frank Sinatra album com-

mercial and a miniversion of FANTASIA to sell shampoo, created the brighly colored SEASIDE WOMAN (1980). Ian Emes' stark film THE BEARD (1980) is drawn in a liney style, very different from the colored animated fantasies he has created for rock musicians like Pink Floyd and Linda McCartney. In addition to commercials, Bob Godfrey has made a number of short films, including DREAM DOLL (1980), done with Zlatko Grgic, which received an Oscar nomination. Before his death in 1978, George Dunning was at work on an animated adaptation of Shakespeare's THE TEMPEST. The fragments that were completed suggest that it would have been an innovative and imaginative film.

OTHER EUROPEAN COUNTRIES

Virtually every country in Europe can claim at least one animation studio, although their production tends to be limited to short films and commercials for internal audiences.

Spain

Despite the work of pioneers like Segundo de Chomon and Fernando Marco, little animation was done in Spain before the 1940's. The best known Spanish feature is Arturo Moreno's THE KNIGHT GARBANCITO (1947).

The splashy, angry graphic style of Geoff Dunbar's UBU (England) captures the brutality of Alfred Jarre's savage characters.

COURTESY OF GEOFF DUNBAR

In SEASIDE WOMAN, Oscar Grillo (England) blends the Caribbean rhythms of Linda McCartney's song with a modernization of the angular look of 1920's cartoons.

© OSCAR GRILLO

Currently, there are about five studios operating in Spain. The largest of them, Pegbar
Productions, has produced television commercials and programs for Great Britain,
Mexico, and the United States. They did a
large part of the Ruby-Spears series, "Fang-
face" in 1978, and in 1979 they co-produced
THE LION, THE WITCH, AND THE WARDROBE with
Bill Melendez's London studio.

Scandinavia

At least one studio or major animator can be
found in each of the Scandinavian countries:
Eino Ruutsalo and Seppo Antilla in Finland;
Punktfilm in Norway; Lasse Lindberg, Per
Ahlin and Tage Danielsson in Sweden; and

Quist Miller, Jannick Hastrup, Li Vilstrup, and
Bent Barford in Denmark. Two series by
Hastrup are probably the best-known Scandinavian films outside of the region: THE
HISTORYBOOK, made in collaboration with Li
Vilstrup, is a collection of vignettes about
western civilization; THE THRALLS tells the history of the lower classes in Sweden. In addition to educational films like these, artists in
Scandinavia regularly produce personal and
entertainment films.

Rumania

The best-known animator in Rumania is Ian
Popesco-Gopo, whose film, A SHORT HISTORY,
won the Golden Palm at Cannes in 1957.
Popesco-Gopo has also worked in live-action;
he now heads the cinema and television
department of the World Health Organization
in Geneva. He was also instrumental in
founding the Animafilm Studio, which produces about 50 short films each year—most of
them educational films for children. In 1966,
Rumania instituted an international animation festival at Mamaia, which was to have
alternated with Annecy in France. The Festival has not been held for several years,
although it has never officially been discon-
tinued.

Switzerland

Swiss animation was founded by two Ger-
mans, Julius Pinschewer and Rudolf Pfen-
ninger; today, there are several small Swiss
studios, grouped around the country's major
cities, mostly staffed by young artists. The
short films and commercials they produce
are rarely seen abroad.

Four frames from a
film entitled POURSUITE
by Swiss animator Robi
Engler.

ASIA AND THE PACIFIC

China

Although the first Chinese animated film was made in 1926, the turbulent political and social history of the country prevented much progress from being made in the art form. Not until after the Communist regime came to power did animation reemerge in China. In 1957, the Shangai Studio—the only animation studio in the country—was established under the direction of the artist Ter Fou. Currently, the studio has a staff of about 500.

While the Shangai Studio has produced more than 200 films, few have been seen outside of China. The most common complaint voiced about these films by non-Chinese observers is that they tend to become mired in propaganda, as titles like Chien Yun Ta's THE RED ARMY BRIDGE suggest. China's most interesting contribution to animation is its adaptation of traditional art forms to the new medium, including paper cuts, ink brush work, and traditional Chinese landscape painting.

With its rich heritage of literature and folk tales, there is no dearth of subjects for Chinese animated films. Zhang Guangyu adapted an episode from the famous novel *Pilgrimage to the West* for his film HAVOC IN HEAVEN. (The film was completed around 1967, but the cultural revolution prevented its being released until 1977.) HAVOC IN HEAVEN relates the story of the Monkey King's revolt against the Jade Emperor of Heaven. The film's graphic style reflects the elegant linear patterns typical of Chinese decorative arts: the graceful curves of the Fairy Maidens who encounter the Monkey King show the influence of drawing styles going back to the Han dynasty.

Ter Fou visited America in 1980 and Japan in 1981, showing films in both countries. As

Three films from the Shanghai Studio (People's Republic of China) reflect the visual styles of traditional Chinese arts: (top) FISHING FOR THE MOON FROM THE POOL, (center) PLAYING THE FLUTE, and (bottom) HAVOC IN HEAVEN.

SAZAE SAN, winner of two awards from the Japanese Cultural Ministry, is Japan's most famous animated television series. It began in 1979 and continues to get high ratings today.

China continues to emerge from its self-imposed cultural eclipse, its animated films may well assume a more significant role in world animation.

Japan

Japanese interest in animation was sparked by the early cartoons of J. R. Bray, which were brought into the country during the second decade of the century. Oten Shimokawa, Jun-Ichi Kuochi, and Seitaro Kitayama drew the first Japanese animated films; many of their stories were taken from traditional folk tales. The first sound cartoon was made in 1933 by Kenzo Masaoka, THE WORLD OF POWER AND WOMEN. The animated films of pre-World War II Japan reflect a strange admixture of oriental motifs and the loose-limbed, goggle-eyed look of Hollywood cartoons from the 1920's and 1930's.

Except for a few films like Masaoka's highly regarded THE SPIDER AND THE TULIP, Japanese animation during the war was channeled into making propaganda films. The first animated features were done at the request of the Japanese Navy: MOMOTARO, THE BRAVE NAVY (1943); MOMOTARO, GOD'S SOLDIER (1944); and FUKUCHAN AND THE SUBMARINE (1944).

After the war, animation flourished and quickly spread to the new medium of television. Tadahito Mochinaga made the first puppet animated films in Japan at this time. Since then, this technique has been used in short films, features, and television programs. Like the American animation industry, the Japanese industry is geared to producing large amounts of material on tight deadlines

and restricted budgets, usually for television. In the last 35 years, Japanese studios created more than 40 features and 200 television shows. In addition, about 400 animated commercials are produced in Japan each year. While some programs have been made in Japan for American television, like KING KONG (1967), the few Japanese-American collaborations, like WINDS OF CHANGE (1980), have not been particularly successful.

There has been no "Japanese Disney" to establish a strong tradition of full animation: Japanese animated films are produced simply, quickly, and efficiently. Most television programs use only about 6 drawings per second, which gives the movements a stiff look. As a compensation, the characters and backgrounds are often highly detailed.

Unlike animation in most other parts of the world, the sound track is recorded last for Japanese productions. The animators read the dialogue themselves to get an approximate timing; the voices are recorded only after the film has been drawn, inked, painted, photographed, and edited. As lip sync is impossible to achieve under these conditions, Japanese animators use only three mouth positions: fully open, half open, and closed.

While the subject matter may vary from an adaptation of Louisa May Alcott's *Little Women* to a science fiction epic, great emphasis is placed on the story in Japan. Stories of family relations and of lovers or heroes battling evil are most popular. One Japanese maxim states "A weeping story is a good story, because it is always appealing." Live-action directors often work on animated features because they are believed to have a better understanding of dramatization. As a result, Japanese features tend to be exciting, well-directed, and well-edited.

The major Japanese studios are Toie Doga, Tatsunoko Productions, Tokyo Movies, Nippon Animation, Dax International, and Cartoon Factory. A number of their characters enjoy an enthusiastic following in the United States and Europe, including Kimba, the White Lion (Mushi); Astro Boy (Osamu Tezuka); and Lupin III (Toie). The characters themselves are designed with an eye toward merchandising, as evidenced by the enormous popularity of the toy robots based on such Toie creations as Gackeen the Magnetic Robot and Mazinger Z. In addition, there are several independent producers who work with various Japanese production companies and advertising agencies in Europe and the United States.

Although animation is taught only at the Tokyo Designer's College, there is a highly appreciative audience for the medium in Japan. There are at least a half dozen animation fan clubs and study groups, and numerous animation fanzines are published there.

Very little independently made Japanese animation is seen outside of the country, but films like Kihachiro Cawamoto's HOUSE OF

Japanese animation varies greatly in style as these examples from ULYSSES (left) and THE ADVENTURES OF BARNABY BEAR (right) illustrate.

© TOKYO MOVIE SHINSA CO. LTD.
© TELECIP/HERSCOVITZ

FLAME (1980) suggest that interesting and artistic work is being done there. HOUSE OF FLAME combines Bunraku puppets with drawn animation to tell a traditional Japanese drama. The overall effect is a striking one that seems more closely allied to the traditional art styles of Japan than the films of its major studios.

Australia

Animation is a relatively new medium in Australia. The oldest studio in the country, A. P. I. (Air Programs International Productions Pty. Ltd.) was established in 1958. Based in Sidney, A. P. I. has done programs for Australian, Middle Eastern, and American television. Probably the best known of their programs is a half hour adaptation of THE SWISS FAMILY ROBINSON, which was nominated for an Emmy in 1973.

Eric Porter Productions created a feature entitled MARCO POLO in 1971, which has been favorably reviewed but rarely seen. The third major studio in Australia is a subsidiary of Hanna-Barbera, which produces animated programs for American Saturday morning television.

More than a dozen small studios exist in Australia; the best known of them is headed by Yoram Gross. This Polish-born animator emigrated to Israel in the late 1950's, where he directed the puppet feature JOSEPH SOLD BY HIS BROTHERS (1959). In 1968, he moved to Australia, where he had made three features that combine animation with live-action backgrounds and/or characters: DOT AND THE KANGAROO (1977), THE LITTLE CONVICT (1979), and SARAH (1982).

In addition, a number of independent animators work in Australia, including Antoinette Starkiewicz, Arthur and Corrinne Cantril, Sonia Hoffman, and Alexander Stitt. The most prominent independent in Australia is Bruce Petty, a commercial artist, illustrator, and political cartoonist. Petty is known for his satirical films like AUSTRALIAN HISTORY (1972) and LEISURE (1977), which won an Academy Award.

The Third World

Relatively little animation is done in the countries that comprise the Third World. Animation is an expensive process that requires highly trained artists, sophisticated production equipment, film laboratories and editing facilities, distribution companies, and theatres. An industrialized economy is needed to support animated filmmaking in any quantity.

The problem is essentially economic, as the artistic traditions of any country are a potential source of animated films, as demonstrated by the work done by the Cape Dorset Eskimos, sponsored by the National Film Board of Canada. These handsome films combine modern film techniques with traditional Eskimo motifs and legends: a rare, happy marriage of native styles and contemporary technology.

The animated films that are produced in Third World countries tend to have limited and brief distribution. For example, few observers have seen Cuba's first animated feature EL PIDIO VALDES AGAINST THE MACHINE GUN, directed by Juan Padron. Equally few outside of the Orient have seen any of the five features done by the Century Co., Ltd. of Seoul, South Korea. Today, much of the animation done in Korea and Taiwan is "runaway" production for American television.

It is regrettable that so little use has been made of the communicative potential of animation to help solve the problems of the emerging nations of the world.

NORTH AMERICA

Canada

Every once in a while, someone gets sick looking at my films, and sometimes a little old lady will call me a communist because she doesn't understand what I'm trying to do, but it's all part of the business.
—NORMAN McLAREN

The dominant force in Canadian animation is the National Film Board of Canada. The Board was established in 1939 "to explain Canada to Canadians and to people of other lands." During the crucial years of World War II, the Board's function was to help unite a small, mostly rural population, scattered over an enormous country. By 1980, the Board had an annual operating budget of over $37 million and employed nearly 1,000 people in its distribution and production facilities, including English and French language animation units.

In 1942, John Grierson, the first film commissioner, invited fellow Scotsman Norman McLaren to establish an animation unit. McLaren agreed, but resigned his administrative duties after 2 years to devote his time to filmmaking. He quickly established himself as one of the most brilliantly innovative and influential filmmakers in the history of animation.

He scratched, painted, and drew images directly onto blank film stock, and created many of the accompanying sound tracks by artificially generating the tiny lines the projector reads to produce sound. In 1952, he created NEIGHBORS, his Oscar-winning parable of human aggression, using the stop-motion technique of pixilation. He used three-dimensional objects, cutouts, and live actors (including a cat) to demonstrate the structure of a musical form in CANON (1964). He pioneered the use of step printing in films like PAS DE DEUX (1967), transforming the movements of the dancers into graceful, semi-abstract patterns.

Grierson promised McLaren artistic freedom—a promise he kept and extended to other filmmakers. Attracted by this freedom—and the chance to work with McLaren—animators have come from all over the world to make films at the Board: Alexander Alexeieff and Claire Parker (France); Co Hoedman and Paul Driessen (Holland); Ishu Patel (India); Zlatko Grgic (Yugoslavia); Bretislav Pojar (Czechoslovakia); Lotte Reiniger (England); John and Faith Hubley and Caroline Leaf (United States). They joined native Canadians like Barrie Nelson, Jacques Drouin, Sheldon Cohen, Janet Perlman, and Suzanne Gervais.

Many of these artists employed new or unusual animation techniques, like paint-on-glass, sand-on-glass, and pinscreen. The many awards that films from the Board have

Norman McLaren at work at the National Film Board of Canada. McLaren remains one of the most innovative and influential frame-by-frame filmmakers in the world.

ELBOWING (Jeu des Coudes) by Paul Driessen (Canada/Holland): an absurd, idiosyncratic world of bizarrely stylized figures that can be interpreted on many levels.

CRAC! (Canada) by Frederic Back: a warm, human story of a rocking chair that provides the focus of a family's life in rural Quebec.

won in recent years—including three Oscars for eight nominations—attest to its ongoing vitality as a creative force in animation.

Since 1968, another goverment-sponsored entity has been producing first-rate animation in Canada: Radio-Canada, the French language arm of the Canadian Broadcasting Company. Under the energetic direction of Hubert Tison, Radio-Canada has produced approximately 1,000 animated films in the last 14 years. Many of these are titles that last only a few seconds, but each year, one or two films of several minutes are made. Paul Driessen made his droll ELBOWING (1979) there; Frederick Back created his Oscar nominee TOUT-REIN (1980) and his Oscar-winning CRAC! (1981).

In addition, a number of independent animators work in Canada. One of the better known is Michael Mills, who created THE HISTORY OF THE WORLD IN THREE MINUTES FLAT, which received an Academy Award nomination in 1981. A major animation festival is held in Ottawa every other year, and the Cinematheque Quebecoise maintains one of the world's most complete archives of materials relating to animation.

United States

The history of animation in the United States is discussed in detail in Chapter 1.

Today, animation in America is split by two divisions: one geographic, the other, aesthetic. While virtually every major city in America can boast of at least one animation studio, the vast majority of animated filmmaking is done either in New York or Los Angeles.

Most of the animated films made in New York are television commercials, although that situation has begun to change in recent years. Increasing numbers of television specials are being produced in New York. Perpetual Motion has done several ½-hour shows featuring the Berenstein Bears. Zander's Animation Parlor's 1-hour special based on the best-selling book *Gnomes* (1980) had a budget of approximately $1 million.

But the bulk of New York production still consists of commercials. Zander's alone does about 100 spots each year; Perpetual Motion, 60 to 70. Other major studios include Ovation Films, Inc.; KCMP Productions, Ltd.; and Kim & Gilford, Inc.

New York animation studios have a talent pool of three or four hundred artists on which they can draw; the West Coast talent pool is closer to 3,000. Los Angeles is *the* center of animation production in the United States.

Jeremy the crow, disguised under a lily pad, greets Mrs. Brisby in THE SECRET OF NIMH, by Don Bluth, USA.

Located in the greater Los Angeles area are the major Saturday morning houses—Hanna-Barbera, Ruby-Spears, and Filmation; many of the studios that produce theatrical features and/or television specials—Walt Disney Productions, Ralph Bakshi, Don Bluth, Chuck Jones Enterprises, Warner Brothers, M. H. V., Bill Melendez; and a number of important commercial houses—Duck Soup, Spung-buggy, Kurtz and Friends, Richard Williams, Pantomime Pictures, Robert Abel & Associates, and Quartet Films, to name but a few. While a minor friendly rivalry exists between the two centers of production, artists can easily move from one area to the other.

The aesthetic division is a more serious one, less easily bridged. In no other country does so clear a distinction exist between animation as an art form and animation as an assembly line product. On one side of this division are the Saturday morning houses that must produce vast amounts of film every year on limited budgets and tight deadlines.

In these studios, the first 3 or 4 months of the year are devoted to developing ideas for shows and negotiating contracts. In late March or even early April, the networks decide what programs they want for the next fall season; the contracts are signed and production begins at a frantic pace. The number of people working at the studios triples or quadruples. Huge amounts of overtime have to be paid as work continues nearly around the clock. Increasing amounts of "overflow" production is sent overseas to be done at studios in Korea, Taiwan, or Australia.

It is difficult to grasp the amount of animation that must be produced: for the 1980–81 television season, Filmation Studio alone produced 76 half-hour programs. Although these shows aren't intended to be masterpieces of the animator's art, this scale of production is staggering. Even at the height of production, Disney, Warners, or MGM never did more than 2 or 4 hours of animation per year.

In the late fall, when the programs have been delivered, most of the studios' employees are laid off, and the research and development phase begins again. This develop-for-four-months/work-frantically-for-eight schedule causes serious economic problems for the animators. This pattern also makes it extremely difficult for a young animator to learn from an older one, or for any sort of *esprit de corps* to develop within the studio. Top quality animation simply cannot be produced under these conditions. However, barring a major

Fat Albert and the Cosby Kids, characters from Filmation Studio's popular Saturday morning program.

HEIDI'S SONG, created by Hanna-Barbera, is the studio's most recent attempt to move from television to feature animation.

Airbrushed imagery for Gilette's BRUSH UP commercial by Duck Soup Producktions.

shift in network policy, this method of production is unlikely to change in the foreseeable future.

At the other end of the spectrum are the independent animators and small studios who use animation as a means of artistic expression. (This work and its significance is described in Chapter 5.) While these artists deservedly win awards in film festivals and earn the respect they command as creators, they face severe economic difficulties due to the meager rentals short films command, the lack of government support for the arts, and the limited amount of animation one artist can do. No independent animator gets rich from his films; very few can even support themselves.

Between these extremes fall the studios that specialize in features or television specials and the commercial houses. The former vary in size from a small group of artists, like Chuck Jones Enterprises or M. H. V. and Friends to major corporations like Walt Disney Productions. Feature studios also face financial problems: a quality animated feature requires an investment of several million dollars; a good prime-time ½-hour special will cost close to $500,000. Production costs continue to rise, distribution is often difficult to obtain, and well-trained animators are perennially in short supply. In addition, there are the aesthetic questions of sustaining story, pacing, and design over a long period of time.

Commercial studios must also face problems of client and agency approval and tight deadlines. While some of the best animation done in America over the last decade has appeared in advertisements, many commercial animators would like to tell a story without having to sell soap or cat food, and to make films that would last more than 30 or 60 seconds.

The early 1980's seem to be a time of flux for American animation. Never in the history of the medium has there been such a widespread interest in animated films, nor so large an audience for them. But rising costs of production and the general economic situation threaten the continued existence of the medium. However, these threats are balanced against the potential offered by such new systems of distribution as the video disc and cable television, and the technological innovations in direct-to-videotape animation and computer-generated imagery.

The challenge that faces American animators is whether they can overcome the problems and take advantage of the new opportunities to create films that will reclaim the pre-eminent place they have enjoyed in animation throughout most of the history of the medium.

ASIFA

One element that helps to link this widely separated group of artists is ASIFA, L'Association Internationale du Film d'Animation. The organization was founded in 1960 by an international group of animators who met in Annecy, France. The original purpose of their meeting was to establish a film festival that would provide the equiv-

alent of Cannes for animation; the result was an international cultural organization. The charter ASIFA received from UNESCO states that its purpose is "to further the art of animation and to promote international understanding through the medium of animation."

Today, ASIFA has chapters in more than 33 countries around the world. The membership is made of up professionals in animation—producers, directors, artists, voice actors, writers—as well as students of animation and private citizens who have no connection with animation other than their love of the medium. Anyone interested in animation may join. ASIFA also sponsors the annual International Tournee of Animation, a traveling program of short films from around the world. Produced by Prescott Wright in San Francisco, the Tournee provides a rare opportunity for people to see examples of the animation done in various countries.

The activities of the individual chapters vary. The parent organization sponsors the world's four major animated film festivals: Zagreb in Yugoslavia, Varna in Bulgaria, Ottawa in Canada, and Annecy in France. Newsletters issued by the various chapters facilitate the exchange of animation news among the international membership.

Within the United States, there are ASIFA chapters in New York, Chicago, San Francisco, and Los Angeles. The New York chapter sponsors an annual film festival, with prizes in various categories.

The largest chapter in the organization is located in Los Angeles. Among its other projects, each year ASIFA-Hollywood puts on two major events: the Annie Awards, in recognition of excellence in the medium, and their Annual Animation Art Festival. The chapter also maintains the only animation art conservation laboratory in the world.

"ASIFA is many things to many people," comments writer-producer-voice actor Bill Scott, president of ASIFA-Hollywood. "We strive to bring each member closer to things that will make animation better. One of our long-range goals in that direction is the establishment of the first animation technical center in the United States."

John Halas, president of ASIFA/International, offers these thoughts on the state of the art form:

"Nobody would dispute the fact that animation has contributed enormously to basic human values during this century, on many essential levels which have influenced the lives of everyone.

"In its first period, animation's major contribution was one of imaginative and carefree entertainment, qualities which made millions of people, from small children to mature adults, elated, delighted, and happy.

"In the second period of its development, animation gradually became an art form. A fundamental means of human expression which gradually but surely expanded the visualization of the subconscious.

"The third period, from the beginning of the 1970's, introduced a new form of image-making through the use of video and computer techniques. This form of picture-making with all its wonderful effects was once again able to echo the early magic of the cinema when animation astounded audiences with its compelling impact, novel ideas, and techniques. With the application of newer technologies, I have no doubt that the same dynamic and explosive growth will take place as it did during the early days of animation.

"As far as the broader applications of animation are concerned, it has a record just as spectacular in its artistic and technical development. Its utilization is enormous, from entertainment to advertising, from science to teaching, from art to experiments; just a few aspects of the wide range of the medium.

"After some 80 years of development, we have today reached the stage when we can be very proud of our contribution to the film and television industries and can also claim to have established a rich tradition for the medium.

"As far as the future is concerned, we can look forward to further progress that animation is poised to make and penetrate further into every sphere of visual communication in order to enrich our society."

For further information concerning the location of the ASIFA chapter nearest you, write to

ASIFA-Canada
C. P. 341, Succ. Post St. Laurent,
Quebec H4L 4V6

ASIFA-Central
7549 North Oakley
Chicago, IL 60645

ASIFA-East
25 West 43rd St.
Suite 1018
New York, NY 10036

ASIFA-Hollywood
1258 North Highland Ave.
Suite 102
Hollywood, CA 90038

ASIFA/International
ASIFA Secretariat
Voroshadsereg u. 64
1021 Budapest
Hungary

ASIFA-San Francisco
Post Office Box 14516
San Francisco, CA 94114

7

Careers In
Animation

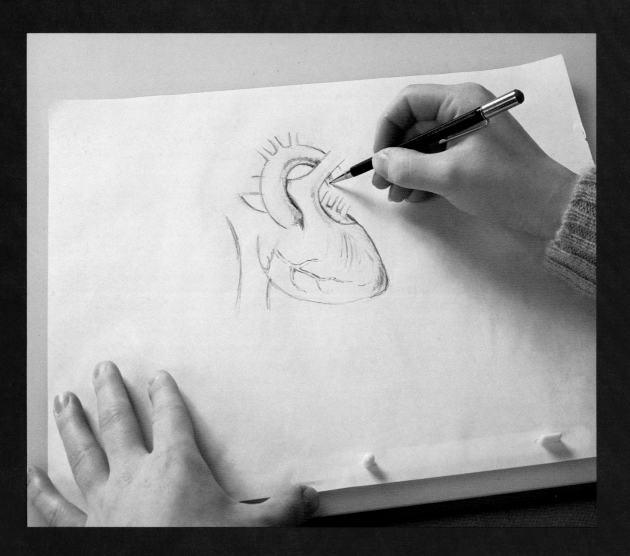

"When I tell someone I'm an animator, the reaction I usually get is 'Wow! I wanted to do that when I was a kid, but I outgrew it.'"
—RANDY CARTWRIGHT, DISNEY ANIMATOR

The idea of planning for a career in animation is a relatively new one. Traditionally, animators have come to the art from other disciplines. Many of the first animators were newspaper cartoonists—men trained to draw characters in ink. A number of famous comic-strip artists experimented with the new medium of animation in the early part of the century, including Rube Goldberg ("Boob McNutt"), Milt Gross ("Nize Baby"), and George McManus ("Bringing Up Father"). The animators who drew the classic films of the 1930's and 1940's came from other backgrounds. Some had studied to become painters, others had planned to be illustrators and do covers for magazines and sheet music. Jobs in art were scarce during the Depression, and many of these artists were hired by the Disney studio during their talent searches of the 1930's.

It is only within the last few decades that colleges, universities, and art schools have added courses in animation to their curricula. Many schools now offer both undergraduate and graduate degrees in animation. Classes in basic filmmaking techniques, including animation, are being taught to high-school and even elementary-school students.

However, an animator is an artist. And a career in animation—like any other art form—requires dedication, self-discipline, and a desire to express something through that medium.

"I don't think of animation as a career, but as an art form, a calling," says Bob Kurtz of Kurtz and Friends. "If you think of it in terms of just a career—a job you might choose like plumbing or engineering—you're in the wrong business. It's something you have to want to do, something you have to be drawn

Bob Kurtz, Kurtz and Friends: "Animation isn't child's play—it's adult's play."

to—you need that special drive. You may stumble into animation from another discipline, but once you discover it, there's never any question of wanting to do anything else."

One point all professionals agree upon is the importance of drawing, especially figure drawing, for an aspiring animator.

"The most common weakness we've found in applicants," states Don Hahn, manager of the Disney School of Animation, "is a lack of the basic skills of draftsmanship: the ability to render a convincing human form with gesture, weight, mass, and construction expressed simply on a piece of paper. That sounds simple, but most of the older animators had that ability because they had literally grown up with a pencil in one hand and a sketch pad in the other. In these days of television, it's hard to find people who have done that."

"Strength in drawing is the first thing we look for," continues Eric Larson, one of the celebrated "Nine Old Men" of Disney and training director for the Disney School. "What does this individual's drawing tell you? Does it make a positive statement? Does it convey a spirit? We aren't looking so much for the finest draftsman as for someone who can make that positive statement."

"There's really only one preparation for animation," agrees three-time Oscar-winner Chuck Jones, "and that's drawing the human figure. A couple of years of life drawing would be a minimum training. Within that context, the artist should acquire control of his line—trimming away the 'fat,' the excess lines—until every line communicates something, and he can live by the line he draws. If you look at art history, every important artist, from da Vinci to Picasso to Claes Oldenburg to Herblock had that sort of control.

"Once you learn to draw, you can go from there—Jackson Pollock could draw beautifully. It's comparable to learning the basics of syntax before you try to write: James Joyce couldn't have written the way he did if he hadn't had an understanding of standard syntax and grammar."

"Preparation for animation?" replies Eric Goldberg, a young animation director formerly with the Richard Williams Animation. "I think there is only one answer: drawing—lots and lots and lots of it. It also wouldn't hurt to have a feeling for a range of graphic styles—not just the standard cartoon style. That can be very limiting. Commercials are a good training ground in that respect, especially in Europe."

But raw drawing ability alone is not a sufficient background for animation: Training and study are also necessary.

"Whether you want to be an animator or anything else in the animation industry, go to school," urges Bill Hanna of Hanna-Barbera. "Schooling gives you a confidence and poise that is necessary for any endeavor."

"I would advise anyone interested in entering the animation arena to attend school," agrees Ralph Bakshi, whose credits include FRITZ THE CAT and AMERICAN POP. "I got a job as a cartoonist right after high school, but in looking back, I would have preferred to pursue my education further first."

Dan McLaughlin, director of the UCLA Animation Workshop, summarizes the varied course of study he recommends to his students:

"Anyone interested in animation should determine as early as possible what it is he or she wants to do and say in the medium and gear his or her studies accordingly. For example, someone interested in stop-motion animation should follow a different curriculum than someone interested in drawing Disney-style character animation, which would be different from what someone interested in owning his or her own studio should study. Once that's determined, it's important to find your strengths and weaknesses and push your strengths: A mind geared toward work and self-discipline is very important in animation.

"Anyone who wants to become an animator should go to college or art school if at all possible, and drawing will obviously be one of the essentials of the course of study. The trick is to find a school that teaches the craft of drawing—that is, how to draw, rather than the philosophy of drawing, which is more traditional. An animator should also take classes in design, perspective, the use of color, various techniques and media, and art history.

"It's also beneficial to take a certain number of outside classes," concludes McLaughlin. "Acting and/or directing is useful, as is dance or mime. A knowledge of computers is going to be increasingly important. Animators should read as widely as they can—the knowledge they gain provides sources for their film work. And a writing class in some short form, like the short story, can provide useful information about elements of structure, style, and form."

While a college education seems to be necessary for an aspiring animator, it is useful, but not vital, for someone interested in entering other areas of the animation industry.

"While I recommend schooling for anyone interested in being an animator," explains Nick Bosustow, president of Bosustow Productions, "many positions, such as camera operator or painter, can be learned on the job. A small non-union studio can train a newcomer in just about any job, little by little, once he's entered the studio as a messenger or general gopher."

"Knowledge of the structure of the human body is the basis of almost all good animation because the movements are modeled after those of the human body," comments T. Hee, whose credits include codirection of the "Dance of the Hours" sequence of FANTASIA; he now teaches caricature at the California Institute of the Arts (CalArts) in Valencia.

"Without the knowledge of anatomy Walt

Dan McLaughlin, independent filmmaker and professor of animation at UCLA: "a mind geared toward work and self-discipline is very important."

Bill Hanna, Hanna-Barbera Productions: "Schooling gives you a confidence and poise."

ensured his artists got and the flexibility it gave them, the Disney films as we know them would never have existed. The artists who drew the classic films like SNOW WHITE had all studied life drawing, either at Chouinard or a comparable art school. Or they were deeply involved in other areas of art—like the architectural drawing needed to create atmospheric backgrounds.

"Of course, there are other skills an animator needs to have," he continues. "Caricature, the ability to create recognizable characters through the use of exaggeration is one. A knowledge of perspective is another. Perspective cannot be handled haphazardly in good animation—it has to be caricatured to allow the character to break loose. Also, an animator should study acting—including dance and mime: He has to understand what's happening during a specific movement and why.

"Most importantly, an animator has to learn how to think. To make a character move properly, an animator has to be able to think as that character."

"Experience is the best training," comments John Dadarian of Animagraphics, a West Coast animation camera service. "Some sort of artistic background and a limited mechanical ability are good prerequisites for a career as an animation camera operator. A camera is just another piece of machinery, except it has film running through it. You need a certain feel for it—you don't have to be able to tear it apart and put it back together, but you need to understand how it works and what its limitations are."

"We generally look for someone with an art school or film-school background," agrees Ray Kerns of Computer Camera Service. "A good film school can provide useful information. But an animation camera operator needs a solid mechanical background and an aptitude for mathematics. The latter is particularly important these days, because a great deal of

work is being done on computerized animation stands. We're not shooting on the old Oxberrys anymore; this is highly sophisticated equipment. We can't afford to give someone the time to reshoot things. The work has to be done swiftly and correctly."

"Anyone interested in becoming an inker or a painter should have an interest in art and some art training," says Judi Cassell, who owns and operates an ink and paint service. "A degree isn't necessary, but the interest is, especially for an inker who may want to move into other areas of the animation industry. Because we use special paints, and the surface of a cel is so different from paper, special training in something like calligraphy isn't of much use. In fact, we prefer to train inkers and painters from scratch. Self-discipline is another important factor—the kind of person who has to jump up every 10 minutes isn't going to be a success in ink and paint."

For decades, the men and women who create animation have been the unsung heroes of film. While a few directors and animators have begun to receive honors and awards, the vast majority of the people behind the films remain unknown to their audiences. For many years, animators did not even receive screen credit. They still aren't paid residuals for the films they draw, although the actors and actresses who provide the voices for the characters are.

But despite the lack of recognition, people in the animation industry speak of their work with a deep and special satisfaction. Few would ever want to do anything else. Wolfgang Reitherman, one of Disney's "Nine Old Men," described the power the medium holds over its practitioners when he said: "Animation is something you can't just *draw*, and that's the beauty of it: You start to get the feeling of a force of nature about it." And Kurtz sums up the pleasures of working in animation when he says, "Animation isn't child's play; it's adult's play."

Nick Bosustow, Bosustow Entertainment: "Many positions, such as cameraman, can be learned on the job."

Ralph Bakshi, Bakshi Productions: "Pursue your education first."

8

Do-It-Yourself Animation
Basic Information and Simple Techniques

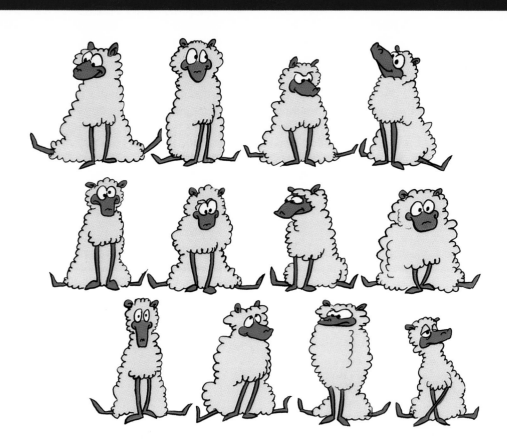

Simple but effective animation can be created using inexpensive materials found in most homes. In fact, some techniques such as flip books and drawing on film don't even require a camera. Making animated films can be a stimulating hobby for an adult, the beginning of a career for an adolecent, or a way of interesting and instructing a child in the basic techniques of filmmaking.

The exercises described in this chapter are elementary ones, designed to give the novice of any age and experience a feel for the basics of animation. However, there is no limit to the sophistication of the animation that can be produced with them. For anyone interested in pursuing animation in greater depth, the books listed in the bibliography can provide more detailed instructions and indicate further directions. In addition, most colleges, many high schools, and even some elementary schools offer basic filmmaking classes, both in their regular curricula and community education programs.

In a first film, the beginning animator should attempt to capture a specific, rather simple, and easily grasped movement, such as a walk, a run, or the bounce of a ball, rather than try to create elaborately detailed drawings or characters or to tell complicated stories. It is normal to want to do everything right from the beginning, but the urge should be resisted. A sense of how and why something moves and how to transmit that understanding through animation should be developed first.

A good animator does not have to be a superb draftsperson. An understanding of how and why people, animals, and objects move the way they do will prove much more valuable than the ability to create a realistic pencil rendering. Careful observation is an important ingredient in developing this understanding.

Gymnasts, dancers, and divers are especially valuable to watch, because their performances dramatically demonstrate how body parts relate to each other while moving, and where key factors such as weight shifts and balance changes occur. A movement reflects the life of its subject—and animation is the creation of the illusion of life.

BASIC EQUIPMENT

Stable supports for both the artwork and the camera are essential since the slightest movement of either, during shooting, will be evident in the finished film. A sturdy table will do for the artwork, and a tripod for the camera. A cable shutter release should be used to prevent any possible camera jiggling during film exposure.

While a tripod will suffice for early experiments and most object animation, serious amateur animators may want to construct their own animation stand for drawn and cutout films. Plans for making the stand illustrated are available for $5.00 from Eastman Kodak Company, Department 642, 343 State Street, Rochester, New York 14650.

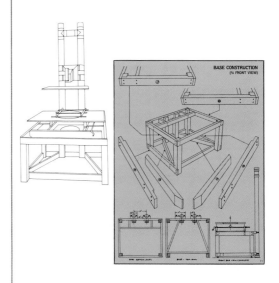

Camera Films for Animation

Name of Film	Film Code No. 16 mm	Film Code No. super 8	Type	Exposure Index	Use	Processing
EASTMAN PLUS-X Negative Film	7231	—	Black-and-white Negative	64	Speed and grain characteristics make this film well suited for general motion picture projection.	Black-and-white with Developer D-96.
EASTMAN EKTACHROME Video News Film (Tungsten)	7240	—	Color Reversal	125	Suitable for television broadcast.	Commercial Labs, Process VNF-1 or RVNP.
EASTMAN Color Negative Film	7291*	—	Color Negative	100	Intended for general motion picture production.	Commercial Labs, Process ECN-2.
EASTMAN EKTACHROME Commercial Film	7252	—	Color Reversal	25	Provides low-contrast originals for color-release prints of good projection contrast.	Commercial Labs, Process ECO-3.
KODAK PLUS-X Reversal Film	7276	7276	Black-and-white Reversal	40	Use with ample artificial illumination.	Commercial Labs, Kodak liquid reversal chemicals.
KODAK EKTACHROME 160 Movie Film (Type A)	—	7245	Color Reversal	160	Accommodates lower light levels and artificial lighting.	This film requires Process EM-25 or *KODAK EKTACHROME* Movie Chemicals.
KODAK Type G *EKTACHROME* 160 Movie Film	—	7248	Color Reversal	160	Accommodates lower light levels and artificial lighting. "No filter necessary" for Type G.	This film requires Process EM-25 or *KODAK EKTACHROME* Movie Chemicals.
KODACHROME 40 Movie Film (Type A)	7270	7268*	Color Reversal	40	Has extremely high sharpness and fine grain.	This film requires Process K-14.
EASTMAN High Contrast Panchromatic Film	5369 35 mm only	—	Black-and-white Intermediate		A laboratory film used for traveling mattes and other special effects.	Black-and-white with Developer D-97

*35 mm format with same characteristics is 5247.

NOTE: Because films are changed from time to time and new ones are introduced, check with a local motion picture film dealer on the latest data if this book is used more than a year after the printing date.

Also, if mixing animation with live action, you may want information on our new high-speed films. Check with a dealer or write to Dept. 642, Eastman Kodak Company, 343 State Street, Rochester, NY 14650.

What Film to Use

Many aspiring artists approach the idea of filmmaking eagerly, only to shy away needlessly when they discover that "film" is not an individual entity, but that there are dozens of kinds of film, each designed for specific uses. Selecting the correct film stock for a project, however, should not be a difficult or confusing proposition. A few simple questions will determine what type of film is best suited to a particular project. A knowledge of photography is helpful, but not vital.

The first consideration is gauge, the physical dimensions of each frame: super 8 mm, 16 mm, or 35 mm. Some feature work is done using 70 mm or special, larger format film stocks, but these are not relevant to the amateur. Each gauge has advantages and disadvantages.

Super 8 is the best gauge for beginners and students through high school, for several reasons. Super 8 is inexpensive and readily available, as is its processing. Many families already own a super 8 movie camera and a projector as well, or this equipment can also be easily rented from a camera or photographic supplies store. A super 8 splicer and splice tabs—precut sections of tape with sprocket holes—can be purchased for a few dollars, and a super 8 animated film a few minutes long can be produced for less than $100. If sound is desired, an animator can do the animation and then synchronize a cassette to the visuals.

There are disadvantages, however, to using super 8. The small size of the frames makes it difficult to edit. Probably the greatest disadvantage is that the finished films can be shown in very few theatres or film festivals. Still, for amateurs just beginning to make films, or making them only for their own amusement, super 8 remains a sensible choice.

Most college students and many independent filmmakers work in 16 mm. It is still relatively inexpensive, the larger size makes it easier to edit, and sound equipment is available. Another important factor is that many theatres and almost all film festivals and contests have 16 mm screening facilities, which increases the chances of a film being seen, winning prizes, or getting distribution.

But producing a film in 16 mm is more expensive than making one in super 8. For example, it costs more to rent a good 16 mm splicer for 1 month than it does to buy a super 8 splicer. A short 16 mm animated film will require a budget of at least a few hundred dollars, and the cost can easily run into the thousands. And 35 mm, which is the standard gauge in the film industry, is even more expensive—beyond the range of most amateurs.

For example: in late 1981, David Silverman, a graduate student at the UCLA Animation Workshop, completed a 5-minute film based on Ogden Nash's poem, "The Strange Case of Mr. Donnybrook's Boredom." He estimates that he spent between $2,500 and $3,000 producing the 16 mm version and making four prints of it. (Approximately $1,000 was spent on an ink and paint service, a step many students do themselves.) To reshoot the film in 35 mm cost an additional $2,500 which covered only the film stock, the camera service, laboratory costs, and four prints.

After determining the gauge in which the film will be shot, the filmmaker must decide whether the film will be in black and white or color. Most animated films are made in color, but black and white can be very effective for animation drawn in pencil, charcoal, or ink on paper. Once you make this decision, the film stock can be selected. The following pages will give you basic information about the various Kodak film stocks available. Kodak also offers free technical advice. For this service, see the listing at the back of this book for the address and telephone number of the representative nearest you. The beginning filmmaker may also wish to consult a film teacher at a local college or high school. Most of these professionals will generously share their knowledge if approached politely.

Since there are dozens of films made by Eastman Kodak Company available, the list has been narrowed down to those that work best for animation. The choices discussed below include only color films because they're more popular, but there are several black-and-white films listed in the chart for those who prefer it.

The fine grain and high contrast of *KODACHROME* 40 Movie Film make it the most popular choice for super 8 animation; it also has the most compatible shutter speed for frame-by-frame techniques. Other filmmakers prefer *KODAK EKTACHROME* 160 Movie Film (Type A) because of its color balance.

For 16 mm films, most film students choose between *EASTMAN EKTACHROME* Video News Film 7240 (Tungsten), *EASTMAN EKTACHROME* Commercial 7252,

KODACHROME 7270, and *EASTMAN* Color Negative II Film 7247. All of these films have qualities that recommend them for specific animation projects. *EKTACHROME* 7240 is color-balanced for television and should be considered for any projects that may be televised; 7240 is usually used when only a few prints of the finished film will be required. *EKTACHROME* 7252 is a commercial film designed to produce numerous release prints. Because *KODACHROME* Movie Film 7270 produces a high-quality positive original, it is often used for personal films when the original may be projected. *EASTMAN* Color Negative Film is most effective where special effects and/or titles are involved and a large number of prints will be needed.

The Laboratory

Once the film stock has been exposed, it is developed and printed by the laboratory. In the case of super 8 film, the printing step is omitted. The original is developed and projected, which makes the process inexpensive. Stores that sell super 8 film and offer processing send the exposed film to large, specialized laboratories, where it is processed in bulk.

For 16 mm or 35 mm stock, usually the process is somewhat more involved. After the original stock has been exposed, it is sent to a laboratory, where it is developed and a workprint is made. This is an inexpensive print, used for editing. (In animation, editing usually only involves cutting out any mistakes made during shooting and making minor adjustments to make sure that the images and the sound track match perfectly; in live-action filmmaking, the editing process is considerably more involved.) After the workprint has been edited, the original stock is cut to match it.

The edited original and the sound track (on magnetic film) are then sent to the laboratory again, where they are combined and an *answer print* is made. The answer print is examined by the filmmaker to ascertain that the colors are correct and the sound has been correctly matched with the picture.

If only a few release prints are needed, they will be struck directly from the original. Because the printing process can cause damage to the original, however, a color intermediate is often made. Many prints can be struck from this intermediate, while the original is preserved intact.

Choosing a laboratory, like choosing a film stock, may seem like an intimidating process to the beginning filmmaker, but careful consideration of only a few points can demystify the selection process.

Filmmakers who live in large cities where commercial and industrial films are made—such as New York, Los Angeles, London, Tokyo—will have the services of large, professional laboratories at their disposal. Residents of smaller cities or towns may have access to only small laboratories, or they may have to ship their films to a nearby urban center for processing.

A major laboratory may occupy most of a city block and run 24 hours a day. While the majority of their business will come from the 35 mm and 70 mm production of major studios, they will also have a 16 mm department. The amateur filmmaker will probably not need many of the specialized services a major laboratory will offer, such as screening rooms and editing facilities. Nor will a large laboratory find it practical to offer a small occasional customer the same service they offer to a regular, large-scale producer.

A small or medium-size laboratory may not be able to provide some of the services of a large one, but they may be able to offer the amateur filmmaker more personalized service. There are trade-offs involved in choosing between a large laboratory and a small one, as there are in choosing between living in a small town or a large city. Certain questions should be borne in mind while selecting a laboratory:

• Does this laboratory have a reputation for handling this type of film well? Do they do much work for amateurs and students? Do they provide prompt service?

The beginning filmmaker can contact other amateurs or the faculty or students of a local film school to determine the reputation of a particular laboratory.

• Are the prices of this laboratory competitive?

Most laboratories have minimum charges for services, usually the equivalent of processing 100 feet of film at so much per foot. For example: It may cost 42¢ per foot to have a work print made; however, the work print of an 80-foot film would cost as much as one for a 100-foot film—$42, the laboratory's minimum charge.

• Is the location convenient?

The saving of a few cents per foot in laboratory fees can easily be cancelled out if the filmmaker has to travel too many miles getting to and from the laboratory. Residents of small towns may also have to figure in shipping charges when calculating laboratory costs.

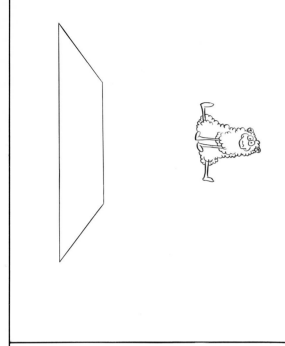

2

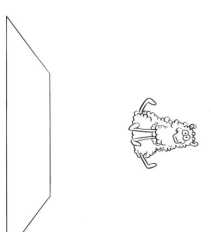

SIMPLE ANIMATION EXERCISES

Flip Book

Materials needed: 3 " x 5 " or 5 " x 7 " unlined cards; pencil, pen, or markers; rubber bands or heavy staples.

The flip book is the simplest form of animation, and requires the simplest materials. Essentially, it is a stack of progressive drawings which are fastened at the side or top and flipped to view the movement.

In his acceptance speech for the 1980 Annie Award, veteran Disney animator Frank Thomas reminisced about how he used to draw flip books in the margins of his high-school text books. File cards are more satisfactory and more lasting. Heavy drawing paper can also be used: a 5″ x 7″ top-bound sketch book can easily be made into a flip book once the covers have been removed. Regular bond paper is too light to flip properly.

Any movement can be used as the subject of a flip book. Beginners may want to start by animating a geometric shape, a stick figure, or a character copied from a newpaper comic strip.

The images are sketched in pencil on the lower one-half to two-thirds of the card: the top third is needed for binding the flip book. Usually, the first drawing in the series will be placed on the bottom page, with the subsequent ones on top of it. Each drawing will be slightly more advanced in the movement than the one beneath it. The relative positions of the images in successive drawings can be checked by using a light table, a light box, or by holding them against a sunny window. The animation can be checked by flipping a drawing back and forth between the ones before and after it to see if the motion is smooth. A drawing may work well within the context of an animation sequence but look

"Sheep Bounce" by David Silverman: a cycle for a flip book. These pages can be photocopied four or five times, and the drawings cut out and pasted onto 3″ x 5″ cards (drawing #1 follows #10). Bind the drawings on the left side. Note the use of squash and stretch as the sheep hits the trampoline and bounces.

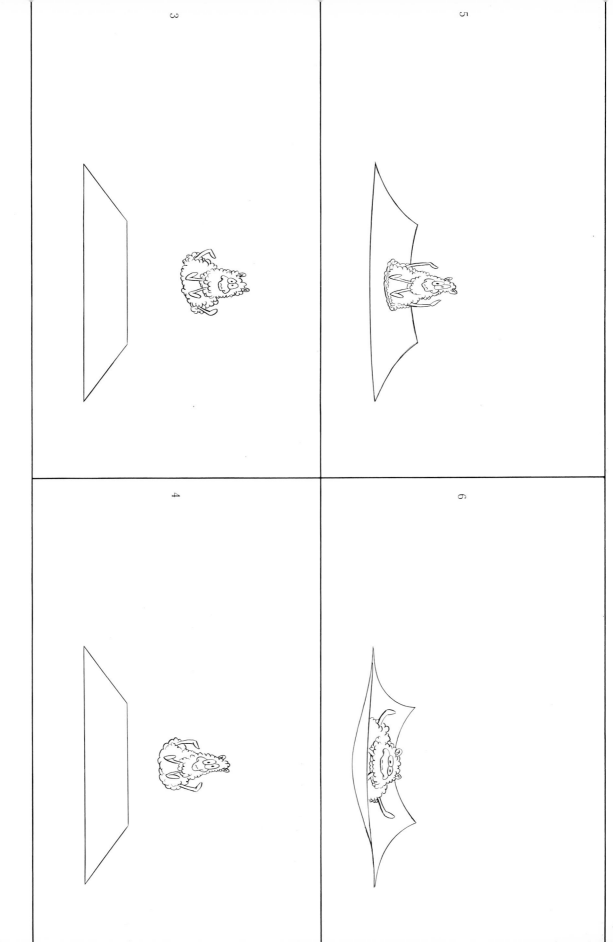

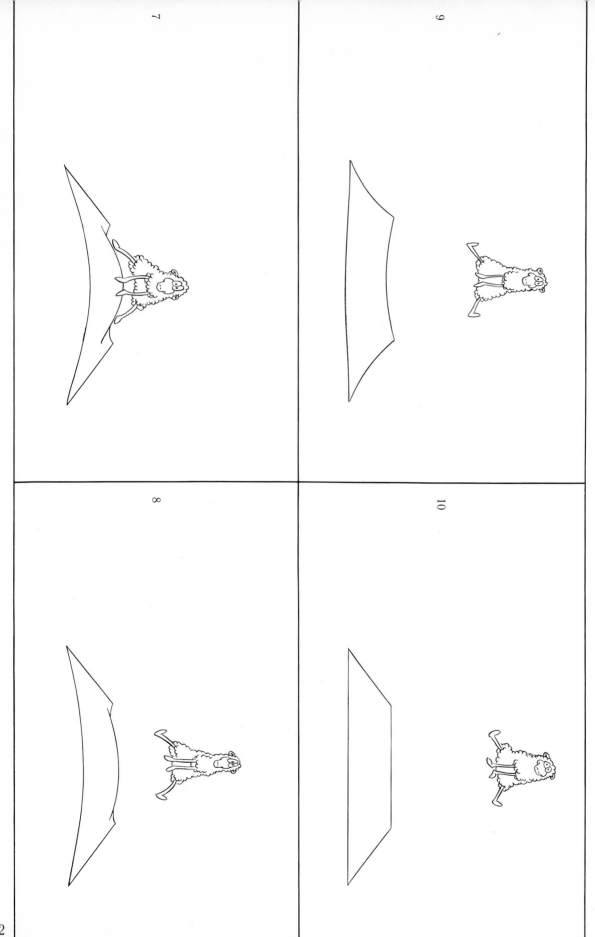

awkward when viewed by itself, as an object or figure may pass through ungainly poses during the course of a movement.

When the motion seems satifactory, the drawings can be gone over in dark ink with a pen or marker, and the pencil lines erased. Forty-eight drawings is a good length for a flip book, and will last for about 2 seconds when flipped. The drawings are bound by stapling one side or the top edges together or wrapping strong rubber bands around them.

A Simple Zoetrope

Materials needed: a strip of light cardboard or plastic, about 3" x 24" with slots ⅛" by 1" cut into one edge at 2" intervals; strips of paper 2" x 24"; pencils, crayons, markers, paints.

The ends of the cardboard strip should be joined securely, and the ring, with slots at the top, should be centered and affixed to the turntable of a phonograph. A cycle of 11, 12, or 13 evenly spaced images should be drawn on a strip of paper and placed inside the cardboard ring. The images are viewed through the slits. The animation will be most effective if the turntable is operated at 45 or even 78 rpm. Shining a high intensity desk lamp onto the images will make them clearer.

If 12 drawings are used, the motion may be rotating or reciprocating; with an odd number of images the movement will be either to the left or to the right. Like the flip book, the images for the zoetrope strips should be bold, simple and clear.

It's easy. Making a zoetrope is relatively simple using strips of paper and a record player.

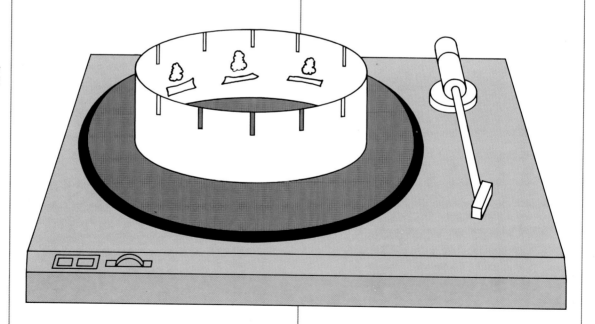

Drawing on Film

Materials needed: EASTMAN Clear Leader 5980 (for 35 mm) or 7980 (for 16 mm); markers or a fine pen and inks made for drawing on film.

Some animation teachers use simple drawing on film exercises to give their students a feeling for the 24-frames-per-second rhythm that is the basis of most film. The artistic potential of this technique was first explored by Len Lye and Norman McLaren (independently) during the early 1930's.

Clear film stock can be purchased at most photographic supply stores or from film-editing suppliers. The inks or markers must say "for drawing on film." These inks are slightly more acidic than normal inks and will adhere to the slick acetate surface of the film stock. Ordinary inks will bead up and slide off the film.

There are two methods of drawing on film. The first involves drawing sequences of tiny images in each frame. To use this method, the 16 mm or 35 mm templates illustrated below should be photocopied and pasted to a piece of wood or heavy cardboard. Pins placed in the sprocket holes will hold the film steady while the artist is drawing. Simple figures, letters, digits, geometric shapes, or patterns of dots are best to use for this type of project. Again, the position, size, or shape of each image should be altered slightly in every frame. Twenty-four images have to be drawn for every second of screen time.

For the second method of drawing on film, long lines or areas of color that overlap the frame lines are applied. These lines and patches will produce abstract designs and motions when the film is projected.

Note: Although super 8 stock could be used for drawing on film projects, it is difficult to find and the frames are so small that it is impractical to use.

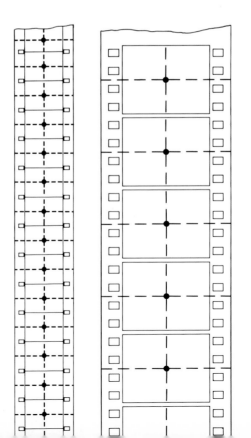

Sequential frames from Norman McLaren's HEN-HOP: while Len Lye completed the first drawn-on-film project in 1935, McLaren has carried the technique further than any other artist.

COURTESY OF THE NATIONAL FILM BOARD OF CANADA

Templates for 16 mm and 35 mm drawn-on-film projects. These templates should be photocopied and affixed to heavy cardboard or balsa wood. Pins passed through the sprocket holes will hold the film in place.

Object Animation

Materials needed: a sturdy table, Plasticene modeling clay, camera and tripod, notebook, ruler, lights.

Simple object animation can be done easily and quickly. A short film can be made in the space of a single afternoon. Figures can be modeled from ordinary children's modeling clay (Plasticene).

The figures should be kept simple; the temptation to make elaborately sculpted figures, with different colored clay for hair, flesh, and clothing, should be resisted. Geometric shapes are probably the best for an animator's first film, with human and animal figures being used in later projects, once the art of manipulating the clay before the camera has been mastered. If the Plasticene figures begin to soften from the heat of the lights, placing them in the refrigerator for a few minutes will restore them to firmness.

If a table serves as a stage for the animated figures, it must be steady, since a wobble will be visible in the finished film. A simple piece of cardboard can serve as a backdrop. Elaborate sets, like elaborate figures, only distract the beginning filmmaker from the real goal of creating movement effectively.

The lights in the room should be checked to see if they provide sufficient illumination for shooting. Many super 8 cameras have built-in light meters, or a light meter can be rented from a photographic supply store. If additional light is required, photoflood lamps can also be rented for a few dollars.

Bob Gardiner's animated mouse, camera, and (next page) man are too sophisticated for beginning students, but show what can be done with the clay medium.

The actual process of animation is deceptively simple: The clay figure or one of its limbs is moved slightly before each frame is taken. A ruler with fine calibrations or a strip of fine graph paper can be used to gauge how far each object should be moved. The filmmaker should keep a record of the movements in a simple log: a notebook with each line numbered to correspond to a single frame (or two frames, if the frame-to-frame difference is very minor). Abbreviations may be used to simplify the process: For example, moving the right leg forward one-quarter or an inch might be noted as *r lg fwd ¼ "*. Changes in camera angle and position should also be noted. Keeping a log may seem like a dreary task, but it enables a filmmaker to determine what rates of movement are most effective when he or she views the film.

Cutouts

Materials needed: Heavy paper or light cardboard, paper fasteners or string, a camera with an overhead mount, sturdy table, notebook, scissors or mechanical artist's knife, ruler, lights.

Because cutout animation can be done cheaply and quickly, it has become a popular method for teaching animation to children. Many professionals also use it because it may require only a few days to complete a film.

The cutout figure(s) should be constructed first. Index cards or the light cardboard sold in art supply stores as railroad board are good materials. Bond paper and construction paper are too light; corrugated cardboard is hard to cut accurately and clumsy to manipulate.

The making of a character: various stages in the clay animation process—rolling out the clay, building the armatured figure, applying and molding the clay on the figure, and the finishing touches. From IMAGES FOR IMAGINATION film segment by Bob Gardiner. Beginning animators should try making characters that are one color, have simple features, and have simple movements.

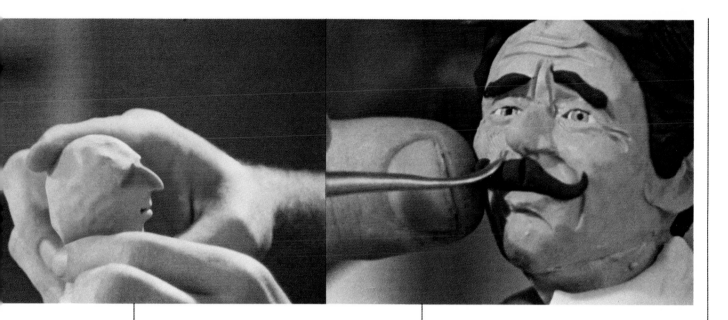

Again, the figures should be kept simple, with joints at the shoulders, hips, elbows, and knees. The joints can be made with either paper fasteners or small interlocking loops of thread.

The figure should be placed on a background on a stable, flat surface under the camera. Again, enough light should be available. As in clay animation, the limbs are moved a fraction of an inch before each frame is taken. The ruler can again be used as a guide to determine the amount of movement. The information should be recorded in a log, similar to the one described in the clay animation exercise.

Making an animated film does not have to be a solo project. Two people or even a group of friends may find they work well together and enjoy the process of filmmaking. Like all arts, however, animation requires concentration, practice, and study if it is to be done well. The beginner should not expect the initial results to look like FANTASIA; reasonably smooth and accurate movement is a sufficient goal at the start.

Making even the simplest film will greatly increase the beginner's understanding of how animation is produced and make him or her a more discriminating observer of other artists' films. Many of the most talented young animators at work today began by creating simple films, like the ones described in these exercises, long before they seriously considered pursuing frame-by-frame filmmaking as a career.

Collecting Art From Animated Films

APPENDIX I

It is only recently that animation has become recognized as a valid art form. It is even more recently that an appreciation of the artistry and labor embodied in every animation drawing and cel has arisen. Major museums, including the Whitney in New York and the Library of Congress, have mounted special exhibits of animation art.

Cels and drawings have become collectibles and often command high prices. The interest in antique dolls and toys and in character merchandise such as Mickey Mouse watches lead collectors to the source of the many objects that featured Disney characters: the Disney animated films. Disney art remains the most sought after and brings the highest prices, but interest in the work of other studios continues to grow.

Art from early animated films is extremely rare. In the days of black-and-white films, the cels were washed to remove the ink and reused. Inking had to be done with a brush, as a pen tended to scratch the surface of the cel, leaving tiny marks when the cel was washed which showed in photography. Cel washer was the lowest position in a studio, but many animation greats, including Tex Avery and Chuck Jones, began as cel washers.

Film was regarded as little more than a toy at that time, and no one saw any reason to save drawings or cels or animated films from destruction. Many live-action films suffered a similar fate: archivists estimate that over one-half of the films made since 1900 have been lost.

When color came to animation in the early 1930's, the studios discovered that the cels could no longer be washed and reused: The colored paints left permanent stains. Like the drawings, the cels were discarded without a thought. Some were deliberately damaged with corrosive chemicals to prevent souvenir hunters from rummaging through studio trash cans. Rumors persist that Disney employees played slip-and-slide on stacks of FANTASIA cels after shooting had been completed.

However, Disney saved the drawings from his films and much of the preproduction material, like story sketches. The studio has literally millions of drawings on file, which the animators use as references. Unhappily, none of the other studios followed Disney's example, and countless thousands of drawings, cels, backgrounds, and sketches were trashed and burned.

Disney was also the first to begin marketing animation art. In the late 1930's, the studio began to market cels, drawings, backgrounds, and story sketches through the Courvoisier Gallery. Later, during the 1950's and 1960's, cut-down cels were sold as souvenirs at Disneyland for a few dollars apiece. Today, those same cels bring hundreds of dollars at art auctions and galleries.

No one group buys animation art. Collectors may buy old Disneyana as an investment; young parents may want a pleasant image for a child's wall; a Beatles fan may be looking for a cel from YELLOW SUBMARINE; a Betty Boop fan may scour shops for an image of the animated vamp; a historian may look for obscure material to round out a personal collection or an archive. A fan of live-action films can collect autographs or stills or posters, but a devotee of animation can own an actual piece of a favorite film.

There is no one best place to buy animation art. Where to look depends on the area that interests the buyer, his or her budget, and knowledge of the field. Art from animated films is easiest to find in large cities where studios have been located, such as New York and Los Angeles. Despite studio security measures, a certain amount of material invariably filters out and into the marketplace. When an old animator dies or retires, materials that were saved may well end up in a second-hand store, a gallery, or an archive. Sometimes material is stolen and resold months or years later.

Certain galleries now deal regularly in animation art. Some of the major ones in the United States are listed at the end of this section. Sotheby-Parke Bernet, the art auctioneers, include animation material in some of their collectibles auctions. These sales are usually advertised in major newspapers in advance. Information may be obtained by writing to them at Sotheby-Parke Bernet Inc., Collector's Carousel, 1334 York Avenue, New York, New York 10021.

In addition, ASIFA-Hollywood sponsors the largest animation art sale in the world each summer, with drawings and cels from current productions and commercials, as well as material from older films. For information on the date and location of this sale, write to ASIFA-Hollywood, 1258 North Highland Ave., Suite 102, Hollywood, CA 90038.

While a rare treasure may occasionally turn up at a garage sale or a curio shop for a few dollars, the novice collector should stick to major galleries or reputable dealers. The rapid increase in the price of animation art has led to the creation of forgeries. A highly trained eye and sometimes a chemical laboratory are needed to detect a well-made fake. The Disney archive will verify that an image comes from a specific Disney picture; write to David R. Smith, Walt Disney Archives, 500 South Buena Vista St., Burbank, CA 91521. The Search & Rescue Team of ASIFA-Hollywood can authenticate animation art from any studio; it is also the only conservator of animation art in the world. Their address is The International Animated Film Society, Search & Rescue Team, 1258 North Highland Ave., Suite 102, Hollywood, CA 90038.

Consideration of a few simple criteria can help a prospective buyer determine whether or not a piece of animation art is a worthwhile purchase. The first point is the popularity of the character and the rarity of examples of that character. For example, the widespread popularity of Betty Boop and the scarcity of materials from the Fleischer Studio would make a cel of her far more valuable than, say, one of Gandy Goose (rare, but not particularly popular) or Scooby-Doo (popular, but not particularly rare).

Next, the aesthetics of the individual piece of art should be examined. Is it a good likeness of the character? Is it a full figure, part of a figure, or just a head? Is the pose dynamic, revealing personality and/or displaying action?

The condition of the artwork should be studied carefully. Is the paint intact, or is it chipped, cracked, faded, or missing in spots? Are the ink lines intact? Is the cel hand-inked or xerographed? Is the cel itself torn or discolored—old nitrate cels will shrink and deteriorate like old nitrate film. Is the condition of the artwork too perfect for its age—after more than 40 years, any cel from FANTASIA should show some signs of aging.

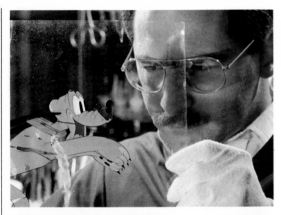

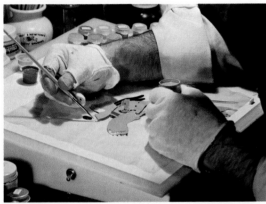

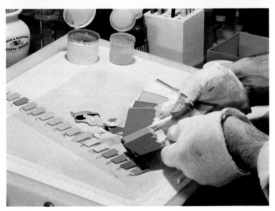

Has the piece been restored? If so, by whom and how extensively? As is true when buying any collectible, nothing should be purchased from a dealer who cannot or will not guarantee the authenticity of the merchandise.

Collecting animation art is by no means the exclusive preserve of the rich. Handsome cels and drawings from commercials, television programs, educational films, and independent productions can be found for as little as a few dollars apiece. Some collectors prefer drawings (which are usually less expensive than cels) because they were done by the animators themselves. Others prefer preliminary sketches and storyboard drawings that offer insights into the creation of a film. The essential criterion for determining whether or not a piece of animation art is worth buying or not is whether it pleases the potential buyer, for whatever aesthetic, historical, financial, or personal reasons.

The following is a selected list of reliable sources of animation artwork, which can serve as a basis for the beginning collector:

Ron Stark (left, top), conservator and director of the Search & Rescue Team of ASIFA-Hollywood, examines a damaged cel prior to restoring it. Restoration of cels is as precise as restoration done on museum paintings and many of the same techniques are used. Shown are two stages of the process: repairing chipping paint (center) and color-matching (bottom).

- Artman
  1620 Valley St.
  Fort Lee, NJ 07024
  (201) 947-1803
- Book City Collectibles
  6625 Hollywood Blvd.
  Hollywood, CA 90028
  (213) 466-0120
- Carolyn Summers Gallery
  505 Altamonte Mall
  Altamonte Springs, FL 32701
  (305) 830-6891
- Carolyn Summers Gallery
  312 Royal Street
  New Orleans, LA 70130
  (504) 523-1350
- Cartoon Carnival
  408 Bickmore Dr.
  Wallingford, PA 19086
  (215) 876-1292
- Cherokee Bookshop, Inc.
  6607 Hollywood Blvd.
  Hollywood, CA 90028
  (213) 433-6090
- Cherry Creek Gallery
  221 Detroit Street
  Denver, CO 80206
  (303) 377-8706
- Circle Gallery
  540 N. Michigan Ave.
  Chicago, IL 60611
  (312) 670-4304
- Circle Gallery
  2064 Prestonwood Town
    Center
  Dallas, TX 75240
  (214) 233-9458
- Circle Gallery
  2895 The Galleria II
  Houston, TX 77056
  (713) 961-7241
- Circle Gallery
  653 N. LaCienega Blvd.
  Los Angeles, CA 90069
  (213) 659-3621

- Circle Gallery North
  1070 Northbrook Court
  Northbrook, IL 60062
  (312) 564-5860
- Clayton Art Gallery
  8113 Maryland Ave.
  Clayton, MO 63105
  (314) 863-3373
- Collector's Book Store
  6763 Hollywood Blvd.
  Hollywood, CA 90028
  (213) 467-3296
- Disney Original Art Program
  Walt Disney Productions
  500 South Buena Vista St.
  Burbank, CA 91521
  (213) 840-1000
- Don Phelps
  71 Esta Rd.
  Plymouth, MA 02360
  (617) 747-0665
- Fantasies Come True
  7408 Melrose Ave.
  Hollywood, CA 90038
  (213) 655-2636
- Gallery In The Round
  Woodbridge Center, Upper
    Level
  Woodbridge, NJ 07095
  (201) 636-7710
- Gallery In The Square
  665 Boylston St.
  Boston, MA 02116
  (617) 426-6616
- Gallery Lainzberg
  417 Guaranty Bldg.
  Cedar Rapids, IA 52401
  (319) 363-6136
- Hi-De-Ho Comics
  525 Santa Monica Blvd.
  Santa Monica, CA 91405
  (213) 394-2820 or 451-0463

- International Animated Film
    Society/ASIFA-Hollywood
  1258 North Highland Ave.
  Suite 102
  Hollywood, CA 90038
  (213) 466-0341
- Museum Shop, The
  2754 East Pacific Coast Hwy.
  Corona del Mar, CA 92625
  (714) 664-4545
- Old Olive Tree Gallery, The
  7136 5th Ave.
  Scottsdale, AZ 85251
  (602) 947-9302
- Old Towne Circle Gallery
  2501 San Diego Ave.
  San Diego, CA 92110
  (619) 296-2596
- One-of-a-Kind Cartoon Art
  775 Livingstone Pl.
  Decatur, GA 30030
  (404) 377-3333
- Owl Gallery, The
  465 Powell St.
  San Francisco, CA 94102
  (415) 781-5464
- Pioneer Square Gallery
  314 1st Avenue S.
  Seattle, WA 98104
  (206) 625-9753
- Promenade Gallery
  215 Promenade Mall
  Woodland Hills, CA 91367
  (213) 884-5314
- Russ Cochran
  202 Aid Ave.
  West Plains, MO 65775
  (417) 256-2224 or 256-2226
- T. R.'s Gallery
  780 7th Ave.
  New York, NY 10019
  (212) 765-6975

Suppliers of Materials for Animated Films

APPENDIX II

Most of the materials needed for an animated film can be found in any reasonably well-stocked art supply store or photographic supply store, although punched animation paper, cels, and vinyl cel paints may be difficult to obtain outside of a major city. What materials a particular film will require will depend on the interests, talent, and budget of the filmmaker. An elementary school child working on a clay film will have no use for an airbrush, but a college student with some knowledge of graphics may find one an indispensable tool.

The suppliers listed in this appendix are well-respected in their fields, and offer assistance to novices as well as experienced professionals.

SUPPLIERS CATEGORICAL LISTING

Animation Supplies—General
Arthur Brown & Brothers, Inc.
Cartoon Colour Company, Inc.
Charrette Corporation
Gomes
H. G. Daniels Co.
Langford & Hill Ltd.
Plaza Artist Materials, Inc.
R. P. Heath Productions, Inc.

Brushes/Airbrushes
Artistic Airbrush Company
Binney & Smith, Inc.
Frisk Products, USA, Inc.
Medea Trading Company
Paasche Airbrush Company
Winsor & Newton

Cameras & Camera Equipment
Alan Gordon Enterprises, Inc.
Crass, KG
FAX Company
Forox Corporation
J-K Camera Engineering, Inc.
Lyon-Lamb Video Animation Systems, Inc.
Neilson-Hordell Ltd.
Ox Products, Inc.
The Saunders Group

Containers
Acon Containers
Loral Packaging, Inc.

Cels
Bourges Color Corporation
Cell-Folia
Langford & Hill Ltd.
Transparent Products Corporation

Editing Supplies
J & R Film Company
Magnasync-Moviola, Inc.

Film
Eastman Kodak Company

Graphic Aids
Bourges Color Corporation
Geographics, Inc.
Tactype

Lighting
Mole-Richardson Company

Paints, Inks & Pencils
Art Color Products, Inc.
Berol, USA
Binney & Smith, Inc.
Cal-Western Paints
Cartoon Colour Company, Inc.
J. S. Staedtler, Inc.
Langford & Hill Ltd.
Palmer Paint Products, Inc.
Salis International, Inc.
Schwan-Stabilo
Vallejo Products

Specialty Products
Tri-Ess Sciences

*Supplier will be glad to supply names of convenient dealers

Supplier	Product or Service	General Comments	Accepts U.S. Funds Only	Foreign Currency	International Money Order	Letter of Credit	Catalog Availability	Product Availability Direct from Supplier	Only Through Dealers*	Dealers and Direct
Acon Containers 7646 Densmore Ave. Van Nuys, CA 91406 (213) 989-2611	Plastic bottles and jars ranging from ½-ounce to 5-gallon capacity	A helpful supplier able to assist with paint and ink storage problems.	●							●
Alan Gordon Enterprises, Inc. 1430 Cahuenga Blvd. Hollywood, CA 90028 (213) 466-3561	Cameras, optics, animation stands, books, projectors, and other motion picture hardware	A major supplier of motion picture hardware; equipment may be purchased or rented.	●				Free		●	
Art Color Products, Inc. 12455 Branford St. #23 Arleta, CA 91131 (213) 897-4635	Vinyl acrylic animation paint	A quality paint supplier with several tones not offered by other manufacturers or dealers.	●				Free		●	
Arthur Brown & Brothers, Inc. Two West 46th St. New York, NY 10036 (212) 575-5555	One of the largest art material suppliers in the U.S.	Products may be obtained both from their retail store and through their mail order department.	●				$2.00		●	
Artistic Airbrush Company 32 NW 11th Ave. Portland, OR 97209 (800) 547-9750	Airbrushes and airbrushing supplies	A mail-order supplier of all types of airbrushing goods. Helpful with problems and advice on methods and practices.	●				Free		●	
Berol, USA Eagle Rd. Danbury, CT 06810 (203) 744-0000	Color pencils and art markers			●			Free		●	
Binney & Smith, Inc. 1100 Church La. Easton, PA 18042 (215) 253-6271	Manufacturers of vinyl acrylic cel paints and fine-point sable brushes		●				Free		●	
Bourges Color Corporation 20 Waterside Plz. New York, NY 10010 (212) 725-0800	Colored cels and graphic aids			●			Free			●
Cal-Western Paints 11748 Slauson Ave. Santa Fe Springs, CA 90670 (213) 723-6362	Manufacturers of vinyl acrylic cel paints				●		Free		●	

Supplier	Product or Service	General Comments	Accepts				Catalog Availability	Product Availability		
			U.S. Funds Only	Foreign Currency	International Money Order	Letter of Credit		Direct from Supplier	Only Through Dealers*	Dealers *and* Direct
Cartoon Colour Company, Inc. 9024 Lindblade Ave. Culver City, CA 90230 (213) 838-8467 or (213) 838-0703	A complete line of Cel-Vinyl® paints and other animation supplies	A major supplier of cel paints, cels, field charts, books, gloves, animation paper, etc, for both independent filmmakers and major studios.	●				Free			●
Cell-Folia Ringbahn Strasse 16 1000 Berlin, 42, Germany 751-5024	Acetate cels		●						●	
Charrette Corporation 31 Olympic Ave. Woburn, MA 01888 (617) 935-6000	Artist's inks, brushes, technical pens, etc	Products are available both through their retail store and mail order.	●				$3.50		●	
Crass, KG Oberlin Strasse 3-4 D-1000 Berlin, 41, Germany 834-3995	Animation camera equipment, punches, and other film-making hardware	Besides offering stock products, this company will manufacture special equipment to suit the animator's needs.		●			Free		●	
DeVilbiss Company, Ltd. Ringwood Rd. Bournemouth, England 8H11 9LH 020-15-71111	Manufacturers of a complete line of high-quality airbrushes and accessories			●	●	●	Free			●
Eastman Kodak Company 343 State St. Rochester, NY 14650 (716) 724-4000	Manufacturers of motion picture film	Eastman Kodak Company maintains sales, technical, and service facilities worldwide. Check your local area directory for the facility nearest to you.		●						●
Fax Company 374 South Fair Oaks Ave. Pasadena, CA 91105 (213) 681-3084	A complete line of animation stands, discs, and other related hardware	Fax has supplied a majority of the hardware used in studios in the U.S.	●							●

*Supplier will be glad to supply names of convenient dealers

*Supplier will be glad to supply names of convenient dealers

Supplier	Product or Service	General Comments	Accepts				Catalog Availability	Product Availability		
			U.S. Funds Only	Foreign Currency	International Money Order	Letter of Credit		Direct from Supplier	Only Through Dealers*	Dealers and Direct
Forox Corporation 393 West Ave. Stamford, CT 06902 (203) 324-7400	Animation compounds		●				Free			●
Frisk Products, USA, Inc. 4249 Old Bridge Atlanta, GA 30338 (404) 448-8132	Masking film and air-brushes		●				Free			●
Geographics Box R-1 Blaine, WA 98230 (206) 332-6711	Transfer lettering for titles and other dry-transfer images		●				Free		●	
Geo. Rowney & Company, Ltd. Post Office Box 10 Southern Industrial Area Bracknell, Berkshire England RG12 4ST Bracknell (0344) 24621	Manufacturers of artists brushes and other fine art supplies			●			Free			●
Gomes Neerheide 1, 2430 Olen-St. Josef, Belgium 421-0506	Retail store offering cels, paper, paint, and other animation supplies			● Belgium Funds Only			Free	●		
H. G. Daniels Company 2543 West 6th St. Los Angeles, CA 90057 (213) 387-1211	West Coast's largest supplier of art and drafting supplies	Products may be obtained both from their retail store and through their mail order department.	●				Free	●		
J-K Camera Engineering, Inc. 5101 San Leandro St. Oakland, CA 94601 (415) 534-9018	Optical printers, stop-motion motor drives, cel punches, animation stands, and other animation camera hardware		●				Free			●
J & R Film Company 6820 Romaine St. Hollywood, CA 90038 (213) 467-3107	Editing equipment and supplies	In addition to their Hollywood headquarters, they maintain retail offices at 416 West Ontario Chicago, IL 60610 (312) 787-0622 636 11th Ave. New York, NY 10036 (212) 247-0972.	●				Free			●

Supplier	Product or Service	General Comments	Accepts — U.S. Funds Only	Foreign Currency	International Money Order	Letter of Credit	Catalog Availability	Product Availability — Direct from Supplier	Only Through Dealers*	Dealers *and* Direct
J. S. Staedtler, Inc. Box 787 Chatsworth, CA 91311 (213) 882-6000	Manufacturers and distributors of Marsmatic® technical pens and Lumocolor® markers		●				Free		●	
Langford & Hill Ltd. 10 Warwick St. London, W1R 6LS, England (01) 437-0086/ (01) 439-2505	Supplier of all animation supplies; papers, cels, paints, discs, etc			●			Free			
Loral Packaging, Inc. 1700 South Hellman Ave. Ontario, CA 91761 (714) 947-3756	Polyethylene film containers	These airtight containers are excellent for storing inks and paints. They are available in various sizes and colors.	●				Free			●
Lyon-Lamb Video Animation Systems, Inc. 8255 Beverly Blvd. Los Angeles, CA 90048 (213) 655-0606	Manufacturers of video animation systems that are now a standard in the animation industry in the U.S.	The Lyon-Lamb video animation system received a technical Oscar in 1980.	●				Free	●		
Magnasync-Moviola, Inc. 5539 Riverton Ave. North Hollywood, CA 91601 (213) 763-8441	Manufacturers of the Moviola® editing machine and magnetic sound-track recorder/player		●		●		Free			●
Manoir International 450 West 169th St. South Holland, IL 60473 (312) 596-7700	Manufacturer of airbrush compressors	Their noiseless compressor has made airbrush use easier and more economical.	●				Free		●	
Medea Trading Company 4903 Glisan St. Portland, OR 97213 (503) 231-0795	Importers of Iwata airbrushes		●				Free			●
Mole-Richardson Company 937 North Sycamore Ave. Hollywood, CA 90038 (213) 851-0111	Professional motion picture and television lighting equipment		●		●	●	Free			●

*Supplier will be glad to supply names of convenient dealers

*Supplier will be glad to supply names of convenient dealers

Supplier	Product or Service	General Comments	Foreign Currency	International Money Order	Letter of Credit	Catalog Availability	Direct from Supplier	Only Through Dealers*	Dealers and Direct
Neilson-Hordell Ltd. Central Trading Estate Staines, Mddx., England TW18 4UU 785-6456	Manufacturers of camera stands, punches, and other animation camera hardware			● British Funds Only		Free			●
Ox Products, Inc. 180 East Prospect Ave. Mamaroneck, NY 10543 (914) 698-0392	Complete animation stand and hardware for super 8 format		●			Free			●
Paasche Airbrush Company 1909 Diversey Pkwy. Chicago, IL 60614 (312) 281-6650	A complete line of airbrushes and compressors	A long-time manufacturer of airbrushing equipment that has become a standard in the animation industry.	●			Free			●
Palmer Paint Products, Inc. 1291 Rochester Rd. Troy, MI 48084 (313) 588-4500 or (800) 521-1383	Manufacturers of vinyl acrylic cel paints		●		●	● Free		●	
Plaza Artist Materials, Inc. 173 Madison Ave. New York, NY 10016 (212) 689-2870	Animation cels, paper, gloves, paint, and inks		●			Free	●		
R. P. Heath Productions, Inc. 1700 North Westshore Blvd. Tampa, FL 33607 (813) 879-1343	Ink, paint, paper, cels, punches, pens, brushes, and all other related animation materials	Mr. Heath is also the author of *Animation in Twelve Hard Lessons* (see Bibliography).	●			$2.00 U.S./ $5.00 foreign	●		
Salis International, Inc. 4093 North 28th Way Hollywood, FL 33030 (305) 921-6971	Manufacturers of a complete line of watercolors and dyes for airbrushing. Also a complete line of black and colored inks.	Dr. Ph. Martin's colors have become a standard in the animation and graphic arts industry.	●			Free			●

Supplier	Product or Service	General Comments	Accepts				Catalog Availability	Product Availability			
			U.S. Funds Only	Foreign Currency	International Money Order	Letter of Credit	Catalog Availability	Product Availability	Direct from Supplier	Only Through Dealers*	Dealers and Direct
Saunders Group, The 67 Deep Rock Rd. Rochester, NY 14624 (716) 328-7800	Manufacturers of cel number tabs and VERTAFLIP®, a camera stand accessory to change camera position from vertical to horizontal without a change in the lens axis		●				Free				●
Schwan-Stabilo 6522 Northside Cir. North Fort Myers, FL 33903 (212) 254-7950 or (800) 221-8134	Colored pencils, markers, fibre pens		●			●	Free			●	
Tactype 127 West 26th St. New York, NY 10001 (212) 924-1800 or (800) 221-5812 (U.S. only)	Manufacturers of dry lettering sheets		●				Free				●
Transilwrap, Inc. 14335 Iseli Rd. Santa Fe Springs, CA 90670 (213) 802-1611 *Chicago Office:* 2615 North Paulina St. Chicago, IL 60614 (312) 528-8000	Supplier of animation cels	This company has become a major supplier of acetate cel material to the animation industry and can assist in providing any special plastic materials. Also import and export.	●				Free				●
Tri-Ess Sciences 622 West Colorado St. Glendale, CA 91204 (213) 245-7685	Supplier of general chemical materials used in the motion picture industry	Small and large quantities are available as well as expert technical assistance.	●				Free		●		
Vallejo Products Fassina 4 Villanueva Y Geltro Barcelona, Spain 893-1842	Manufacturers and suppliers of vinyl acrylic animation paints			● Spanish Funds Only			Free		●		
Winsor & Newton 555 Winsor Dr. Secaucus, NJ 07094 (201) 864-9100	Manufacturers of brushes, watercolors, dry-ground pigments, drawing inks, and other artists materials		●				Free			●	

*Supplier will be glad to supply names of convenient dealers

Selected Bibliography

Animation remains the least documented of art forms. Very few books have been written on the subject, and many of those are unreliable for a variety of reasons. Some were carelessly or inadequately researched; others are little more than gushing valentines to favorite studios or directors from adoring fans; some are no more than compilations of studio flack and puffery. To date, no one has published a history of Warner Brothers animation, despite the continuing popularity of their cartoons. Similarly, the stories of UPA, MGM, and the National Film Board of Canada remain unchronicled. No biographies exist of J. Stuart Blackton, Winsor McCay, Otto Messmer, or Vladimir "Bill" Tytla.

Several veteran animators are said to be at work on how-to-animate manuals, but when and if any of these books will be completed is uncertain—some of them have been "in the works" for years, if not decades.

The books listed below are essentially reliable and readily available. All of them are still in print at this writing. Except for the two noted with an asterisk (*), which must be ordered directly from the publishers, any good bookstore should be able to order any of them not in their current stock.

1. How-to-Animate Books

Blair, Preston. *Animation.* (Walter T. Foster, paperback). Blair is best known for his animation of the slinky "Red" character in such Tex Avery cartoons as RED HOT RIDING HOOD. This inexpensive and deceptively simple-looking book contains a great deal of useful information, particularly the section on various types of walks and how to animate them. A standard reference for animation students, it can usually be found in art supply stores.

Bourgeois, Jacques; Hobson, Andrew; and Hobson, Mark. *Simple Film Animation With & Without A Camera.* (Sterling, paperback). Although many of the exercises in this book were designed for children, they can be equally instructive for an adult curious to try animation. Most of the projects can be done inexpensively, using easily obtained materials. Brightly colored and approachable, this book is an excellent choice for a creative child interested in filmmaking.

Dohler, Don, editor. *Stop Motion Animation*.* (Cinema Enterprises, 12 Moray Court, Baltimore, MD 21236). This ambitious pamphlet covers the basic steps of stop-motion animation, from constructing an armature to combining footage of the puppet with live-action backgrounds. The text requires a thorough grounding in film techniques and is aimed at the experienced amateur filmmaker who wants to make his own science fiction movies with aliens and monsters.

Heath, Bob. *Animation in 12 Hard Lessons.* (Heath Productions, paperback). Heath, who designed and animated the Oscar-winning short THE CRITIC, offers a great deal of how-to information in this oversized paperback. The emphasis, however, is on drawing, and it is interesting to compare and contrast his instructions with Blair's.

Laybourne, Kit. *The Animation Book.* (Crown, paperback). Laybourne's lavishly illustrated book is the best how-to manual on animation available. It is structured around a series of exercises designed to provide the reader with a minicourse in animation techniques. Some of the methods described, like paint-on-glass, are highly sophisticated and too tricky for a beginner, but most of the lessons can be done relatively easily and cheaply.

Reiniger, Lotte. *Shadow Puppets, Shadow Theatres and Shadow Films.* (Plays, Inc.) Reiniger, the unchallenged master of the shadow film, shared many of her secrets in this handsome book. Plans for shadow puppet theatres are included along with advice on making shadow films. The tone is friendly, informative, and readily approachable.

Wentz, Budd. *Paper Movie Machines.* (Troubador Press, paperback). Provides cut-and-paste patterns for such early animation toys as the phenakistiscope and the flip book. While these gadgets will delight children, they also offer adults insights into the devices that preceded the animated film.

2. Books on Animation History and Aesthetics

Canemaker, John. *The Animated Raggedy Ann & Andy. An Intimate Look at the Art of Animation: Its History, Techniques and Artists.* (Bobbs-Merrill). This is an excellent general book on studio animation. Well-written, carefully researched and thorough, it offers an inside look at the production of a studio feature. Because Canemaker also worked on the film, he was able to include insights and details not usually available to the general public, including a number of the animators' caricatures of each other. Unfortunately, the final version of the film fails to justify Canemaker's enthusiasm for the project.

Griffin, George. *Frames: Drawings and Statements by Independent Animators.* (Metropolis Graphics, 28 East 4th St., New York, NY 10003). Offers an all-too-rare overview of the work of several independent animators currently working in America. While intriguing as an album of drawings and stills, the book has less impact than it should, because no notes or commentaries on the artists' works are provided.

Maltin, Leonard. *Of Mice and Magic.* (McGraw-Hill). A considerable amount of information has been brought together here for the first time in readily accessible form, but it is marred by minor errors and occasional questionable judgments. This is really a history of the theatrical cartoon short, which is not the same thing as a history of animation. The book ends with the demise of the studio system in the late 1950's/early 1960's; no mention is made of the new studios that have arisen since then, nor of independent or avant-garde filmmakers.

Peary, Gerald and Peary, Danny, eds. *The*

American Animated Cartoon: A Critical Anthology. (Dutton, paperback). Like so many anthologies of essays from various sources, this collection is definitely a mixed bag. The historical pieces by John Canemaker, John Ford, and Richard Thompson are informative and interesting. Animators like Art Babbit, I. Klein, and George Griffin offer rare insights into the mind of the animator at work.

Russett, Robert and Starr, Cecile. *Experimental Animation.* (Van Nostrand Reinhold, paperback). The only book devoted to this interesting area of frame-by-frame filmmaking. Early figures like Oskar Fischinger, Lotte Reiniger, Len Lye, and Norman McLaren are included along with contemporary artists like Frank Mouris, John Whitney, and Robert Breer. Although advances in styles and technology have rendered the book a bit out of date (especially the sections on computer animation), these profiles, interviews, and illustrations provide information that cannot be found elsewhere.

Thomas, Frank and Johnston, Ollie. *Disney Animation: the Illusion of Life.* (Abbeville). The definitive book on the subject. The authors, two of the celebrated "Nine Old Men" from the Disney studio, combine anecdotes and personal reminiscences with discussions of the ideas and techniques that set the work done at Disney apart from that of other studios. Oversized and beautiful, with more than 400 color illustrations and thousands of sequential drawings, this book is a must for any animation library.

Wilson, S. S. *Puppets & People: Large-Scale Animation in the Cinema.* (Barnes). Wilson offers a rare, sane look at the techniques used to create movie monsters, from the classic KING KONG to the low-budget sci-fi film. This is not a how-to-guide, but an explanation of basic film techniques for the viewer who wants a better understanding of terms like "traveling matte," "blue screen," and "composite shot."

Glossary

NOTE TO THE READER: Words printed in capitals refer to entries elsewhere in the glossary, as do references of the type "See INK AND PAINT."

Acetate An abbreviation for "cellulose acetate," a clear plastic material from which CELS are made. Also used as a base for film.

Action The movement of the subject within the camera's field of view.

Anamorphic Lens A special lens that enables a wide-screen picture to be economically shot on a smaller format film. The lens compresses or "squeezes" the image vertically as it is photographed; a compatible lens on the projector reverses the process, or expands the image, producing correctly proportioned images on the screen.

Animation A general term that describes a wide range of FRAME-BY-FRAME filmmaking techniques in which the illusion of motion is created, rather than recorded. Derived from the Latin *anima,* meaning "life" or "soul."

Animation Camera A motion picture camera with single frame and reverse capabilities for animation work; mounted on a CRANE over the COMPOUND.

Animation Disc A disc, of steel or heavy aluminum, mounted over a circular opening in the surface of a drawing table. A sheet of frosted plastic or glass is set into the disc. Light from a fixture below the surface shines through the glass, enabling the animator to see his drawings through several sheets of paper at once. PEGS are affixed to the disc to hold the drawing paper in REGISTER. Because the pegs hold the paper stationary, the disc rotates 360 degrees so that the animator is always working at a comfortable angle.

Animator An artist who uses the techniques of FRAME-BY-FRAME filmmaking to give his artwork the illusion of movement. In STUDIO ANIMATION, the person responsible for drawing the moving characters; in INDEPENDENT ANIMATION, the animator is generally responsible for all phases of production.

Answer Print The first print of a film in RELEASE form, prepared by the LABORATORY for the PRODUCER for acceptance, and when approved, used as a standard for all subsequent prints.

Anticipation A pause or small countermove made by a character in preparation for a major movement; used by animators to help give the illusion of a body moving with the proper sense of weight and balance.

Armature A jointed, metal skeletal structure onto which the figure of an animated PUPPET is built, providing support and shape for the figure, as well as the ability to be properly manipulated.

Assistant Animator In STUDIO ANIMATION, the artist responsible for the drawings that fall between the EXTREME points of a movement. See also IN-BETWEENS and KEY ANIMATOR.

Atmosphere Sketch A quick sketch, generally in color, made by the DIRECTOR or LAYOUT artist, to indicate the mood or style of a scene.

Background A flat piece of artwork that serves as the setting for the animated action, and which may vary from a realistically rendered scene to a sheet of colored paper. Abbreviated as BG or BKG.

Bar Sheet A printed form, used by DIRECTORS and ANIMATORS in planning the movement of art and camera, on which all the elements of a film—music, voices, sound effects, visuals—are charted FRAME-BY-FRAME in their relationship to time.

Bottom Lighting When the source of illumination for photographing a scene comes from beneath the artwork, rather than above it; used for a variety of reasons, such as the creation of glowing letters or stars, or to photograph several layers of drawings at once for a PENCIL TEST. Also known as Underlighting.

Camera Operator The person responsible for translating the instructions on the EXPOSURE SHEET into camera moves and photographing the artwork.

Cel A thin, flexible, transparent sheet of ACETATE, which has been PUNCHED, onto which the animators' finished drawings are transferred—either by inking or XEROGRAPHY—and painted. The clear cel does not show when photographed, so when it is placed over the BACKGROUND, the characters appear to be within the setting.

Cel Animation An animation technique in which the figures to be animated are drawn and painted on cels, placed over a BACKGROUND, and photographed frame by frame. Cel animation has been the standard technique for STUDIO ANIMATION since its invention in 1915.

Celluloid See CEL.

Character Animation The art of making an animated figure move like a unique individual; sometimes described as acting through drawings. The animator must understand how the character's personality and body structure will be reflected in its movements.

Check The step in production in which all elements of a scene are examined and checked against the EXPOSURE SHEET to ensure they are correct before being filmed. In STUDIO ANIMATION, the person responsible for this step is the Checker.

Clay Animation An animation technique involving the use of pliable clay figures that are manipulated before each exposure.

Cleanup The process of retracing the animators' rough, sketchy drawings and converting them into finished drawings with smooth outlines that can be transferred to cels. In STUDIO ANIMATION, this is done by the Cleanup Artist. See also ROUGHS.

Click Track A timing device used when elements of the sound track are added after the animation has been completed. The beat to which the animation is matched is recorded onto tape and played through earphones for the conductor, sound effects creator, and/or VOICE ARTISTS, enabling them to match their sounds to the film.

Color Model A representative drawing or CEL of a character, with all of the colors labeled, that serves as a reference for the PAINTERS.

Color Test Footage of a film that has been timed and which is used as a check to make sure that colors, characters, and backgrounds do not clash in the finished film. See TIMING.

Composite Print A print of a film that contains both picture and sound track. Films regularly shown in theatres are composite prints. Also called Release Print.

Compound The flat, tablelike part of an animation STAND, on which the artwork rests while it is being photographed.

Computer Animation A field of animation that takes advantage of the computer's ability to direct and generate a video image based on preprogrammed input.

Computerized Animation Stand A specialized animation STAND that allows all camera moves to be preprogrammed and activated when the shutter is pressed, permitting greater accuracy and speed in filming.

Crane The mounting that supports the camera over the COMPOUND.

Cut 1) A direct or immediate transition from one scene to the next. 2) The removal of unwanted footage from a film during editing.

Cutouts An animation technique in which small, flat, jointed figures, usually made of heavy paper, are placed over a BACKGROUND and manipulated under the camera, then photographed.

Cutouts on Cels An animation technique combining the cel and CUTOUT methods. The cut out figures are pasted onto cels, placed over a BACKGROUND, and photographed.

Cycle A series of drawings that are photographed again and again. The last drawing moves logically into the first, to create the appearance of continuous, repetitive motion. Cycles are normally used for movements that are repeated without variation, such as walks or runs.

Dailies A print of the previous day's shooting, used to check the results for correctness. Used mainly in FEATURE production. Also called Rushes.

Designer In STUDIO ANIMATION, the person responsible for the overall look and style of the film.

Dialogue The portion of the sound track that is recorded by the VOICE ARTISTS and spoken by the characters on the screen.

Director In STUDIO ANIMATION, the creative head of the film, responsible for the concept of how the SCRIPT will be portrayed, and conveying that concept to the people involved; the unifying artistic force of the production.

Dissolve A camera effect in which one scene gradually FADES out as another simultaneously fades in to replace it. Dissolves are commonly used as scene transitions in animation.

Drawn-On-Film An animation technique in which the image is drawn, painted, or scratched directly on the film stock.

Drawn-On-Paper An animation technique in which the animator's drawings are photographed, rather than transferred to cels. Some artists prefer this technique because they feel it gives them a chance to make a more immediate and personal statement or because the look of the drawing style may be suited to the film's content. The drawings may be done in a variety of media—pencil, pen and ink, pastels, charcoal, etc.

Dry Brush A painting technique in which the brush is dipped in paint, brushed against some unneeded surface to remove most of the paint, then used to produce brush strokes with a rough, grainy, irregular look. Used on cels to create such effects as speed lines, and on paintings for such textures as wood grain.

Edit To arrange the various SHOTS, SCENES, and SEQUENCES, or the elements of the sound track, in the order desired to create the finished film.

Effects Animation The animation of non-character movements, such as rain, smoke, lightning, or water.

Exaggeration The overstatement or broadening of a gesture so that it is perceived clearly by the audience. An essential element of CHARACTER ANIMATION, as the subtleties possible in live-action become lost or appear weak when animated.

Exposure The subjection of a piece of film to light to produce a latent image on the emulsion; to take a photograph. Can also refer to the lens opening (f-stop) and shutter speed.

Exposure Sheet The FRAME-BY-FRAME instructions for the CAMERA OPERATOR that accompany the artwork when it is sent to be photographed.

Extremes Drawings of the key or extreme points of a movement, for example, where weight shifts, balance changes, or the greatest SQUASH and STRETCH occurs. In POSE-TO-POSE ANIMATION, the extremes are drawn by the KEY ANIMATOR; an ASSISTANT ANIMATOR draws the IN-BETWEENS, the action that falls between the extremes.

Fade A camera effect in which the image either gradually appears from black (Fade-In) or disappears to black (Fade-Out).

Feature A full-length animated film, usually 60 to 120 minutes in length.

Field The area that will be photographed by the camera for a given shot and, therefore, the area in which the animator draws. The largest field in standard use is the 12-field (12″ x 9″); the smallest is the 4-field (4″ x 3″).

Field Guide A PUNCHED sheet of heavy acetate printed to indicate the sizes of all standard FIELDS which, when placed over the artwork, indicates the area in which the ACTION will take place. Used by the DIRECTOR, ANIMATORS, and CAMERA OPERATOR to check the size of the area the camera will photograph. Also known as Field Chart.

Flip A method used by animators to check the effect of their work at the pencil stage. The drawings are held at the top with one hand and released sequentially with the thumb and forefinger of the other.

Flip Book A small booklet of sequential drawings that appear to move when thumbed through.

Footage A method of measuring film length and, therefore, screen time. As 90 feet of 35 mm film equal one minute of screen time, 35 mm footage is used in many studios as a measure of an animator's weekly output. Animators also refer to the length of scenes in feet, rather than in seconds or minutes—a 30-foot scene, rather than a 20-second one.

Frame An individual photograph on a strip of film. When the film is projected, each frame is actually seen for one twenty-fourth of a second.

Frame-By-Frame Filming in which each FRAME is exposed separately, as the object being photographed must be altered before each exposure in order to create the illusion of movement in the finished film; as opposed to the more usual method of filming in which the film runs through the camera at a steady, prescribed rate to record action taking place before it.

Frame Counter A digital counter attached to an animation camera which automatically records the number of FRAMES that have been shot.

Full Animation Animation that depicts movement and character as completely and smoothly as possible, giving the illusion of weight and motion in three dimensions. The object in motion is usually completely redrawn for each FRAME. See also LIMITED ANIMATION.

Gauge Refers to the format of the film stock, i.e., super 8, 16 mm, or 35 mm.

Hold To freeze or stop the action. To achieve a hold in animation, the same cel or position of an object is photographed for several FRAMES.

Hot Spot An area of a cel that is reflecting the lights back into the camera, causing that spot to be overexposed.

In-Betweens The drawings that fall between the extreme points of a movement. In STUDIO ANIMATION, these drawings are done by an ASSISTANT ANIMATOR or In-Betweener. See also EXTREMES.

Independent An animator who chooses not to be part of a studio, but works alone to produce his or her films.

Ink and Paint 1) The step in CEL ANIMATION in which the animators' drawings are transferred to cels for photographing; 2) in a studio, the department that performs this function. The drawings are first inked, by tracing them onto the front of the cels with a pen or fine brush, or transferred by a XEROGRAPHIC process. The backs of the cels are then painted, usually with special acrylic paints. Traditionally, this delicate work was one of the few jobs in the animation industry reserved for women; however, today both men and women perform these jobs.

Inker The person who traces the animators' drawings onto cels. See INK and PAINT.

Interlock A system that electronically links a projector with a sound recorder; used during POSTPRODUCTION to view the EDITED film and sound track, to check timing, pacing, SYNCHRONIZATION, etc.

Internegative A negative made directly from the original film.

Key Animator In STUDIO ANIMATION, the artist who draws the key or EXTREME poses; a full-fledged animator.

Key Drawing A drawing showing the most indicative pose in a scene.

Key Pose The characteristic or main pose in a movement. See EXTREMES.

Kinetoscope An early filmstrip device developed and devised by Thomas Edison and W. K. L. Dickson.

Laboratory A facility that specializes in processing and printing film, sometimes offering additional services such as EDITING and film storage.

Layout A detailed drawing of a shot in which background elements, staging of the ACTION, and camera moves are carefully worked out and plotted; the stage of production in which these are determined. See also SCENE PLANNER.

Level Because individual elements or characters in a scene may move at different rates or be drawn by different animators, they may be put on separate cels for ease or economy of animation. The layers of cels are referred to as levels. In some cases, elements of a single character may be animated on different cel levels, for example, the flapping wings of a bird may be on the top level, the body on the second, and the opening and closing beak on the third. Usually the elements that move most frequently will be placed on the upper levels, making it easier for the CAMERA OPERATOR to change them.

Light-On-Dark An inking technique sometimes used to delineate very dark areas on a character, in which the ink lines are a slightly lighter color, adding definition and depth.

Limited Animation A term used to describe animation in which full movement is not depicted, but which relies on KEY POSES and the movement of only those portions of the character that are essential to the motion. Because limited animation can be done more cheaply and quickly than full animation, it is widely used for television shows; however, some animators use it for aesthetic reasons. See also FULL ANIMATION.

Lip Sync An abbreviation for "lip synchronization," the matching of the characters' mouth movements to the recorded DIALOGUE on the sound track.

Looping A process for replacing a portion of the recorded sound track that may be unclear or require changing.

Magic Lantern The first projection device, invented in the 17th Century by Athanasius Kircher, consisting of a metal box with a hole in one side covered by a lens; an image painted on a glass slide placed behind the lens is projected by means of a lamp inside the box.

Mag Track An abbreviation for "magnetic sound track." Sound recordings are transferred to magnetic film during production from ¼″ audiotape, making it easier to synchronize the sound and visuals: A 5-foot scene of the picture requires exactly 5 feet of sound track on magnetic film.

Mix To combine the various sound tracks—DIALOGUE, music, sound effects—into a single track.

Model Sheet A series of drawings of a character showing how it is constructed, its size relative to other characters and objects in the film, and how it appears from various angles and with various expressions. Used as a reference by animators to make sure the characters have consistent appearances throughout the film.

Moviola A trademarked name for a machine with a small rear-projection screen and the capacity to play back several sound tracks. Used in EDITING and for reviewing portions of the film during production. Also used to synchronize or interlock picture and sound track in editing. Newer devices called "flat-bed viewers" are slowly replacing the upright Moviolas.

Multipass To expose the same piece of film two or more times during filming, usually to produce semitransparent effects, such as clouds or shadows.

Multiplane Camera A special animation STAND developed at the Disney studio and first used in *The Old Mill* in 1937. The background artwork is divided into foreground, middle, and distant elements and painted on sheets of glass placed several inches apart. During TRUCKING or PANNING moves, the background elements move in relation to each other, creating an illusion of realistic depth and perspective.

Mutoscope A viewing machine, manufactured in 1895 by the American Mutoscope Company, which used the "flip book" principle to create the illusion of movement. It contained a series of continuous photographs arranged on a horizontal axis. A coin was dropped into the machine to operate the hand-crank that moved the pictures rapidly and created the illusion of movement.

Narration The off-screen commentary for a film; often referred to as "voice-over."

Object Animation An animation technique, similar to PUPPET ANIMATION, in which objects are made to appear to move by manipulating them slightly before each exposure. In this technique, the object animated retains its identity and is recognizable as itself.

On Ones, Twos, or Threes Refers to the number of FRAMES each drawing is HELD during filming. The smoothest animation is done on ones and twos, which means 24 or 12 drawings are used per second of screen time. Animating on threes will work for some movements; if the drawings are held for more than three frames, the movements will appear jerky or stiff.

Opaquing Another term for cel painting, used primarily in the eastern United States; a PAINTER is referred to as an Opaquer.

Original The film on which the picture was actually shot.

Overlay A technique in CEL ANIMATION in which foreground elements of the setting are painted on a cel and placed over the characters to give an illusion of depth to the scene.

Painter The person responsible for coloring in the inked drawings on a cel with paint. See INK and PAINT.

Pan A camera move in which the camera appears to move horizontally or vertically, usually to follow the action or scan a scene. In ANIMATION, the effect is achieved by moving the artwork under the camera.

Pan Chart The charted camera calibrations affixed to the top of the artwork for a PAN.

Panning Peg Bars Specialized moveable PEGS on the COMPOUND, calibrated and controlled by dials, which allow the artwork to be moved to accommodate moving shots such as PANS. Also called Traveling Peg Bars.

Pan Shot Derived from "panoramic." A shot which encompasses a wider area than can be viewed by the camera at one time, and which will be scanned by the camera by means of PANNING.

Pantograph A pointer attached to the COMPOUND which moves over a FIELD GUIDE to indicate the exact position of the compound during an off-center PAN or TRUCK.

Path of Action The movement of a character through a scene; used in LAYOUT.

Pegs Small metal or plastic projections that are affixed to all surfaces that will support the artwork during production. They correspond to holes PUNCHED in drawing paper, cels, and background artwork, and are used to maintain REGISTRATION through all stages of production. First used by Raoul Barré in 1913, and further developed (and patented in 1915) by Earl Hurd and John Randolph Bray.

Pencil Test A film of the animators' pencil drawings, used during production to check the timing and smoothness of the animation. In recent years, videotape has generally replaced film for this use because of its immediacy.

Persistence of Vision The ability of the eye to perceive a series of rapid still images as a single moving image by retaining each impression on the retina for a fraction of a second, thus overlapping the images. This phenomena makes it possible to see the sequential projected images of a motion picture as life-like continuous movement.

Phenakistiscope An early animation device that uses a disc with sequential drawings around its border in front of a mirror to create the illusion of motion.

Photokinestasis An animation technique in which an illusion of movement is achieved by moving static artwork—usually photographs, collages, or reproductions of paintings—under the camera. Also called Kinestasis and Photokinesis.

Pinscreen An animation technique invented by Alexander Alexeieff and Claire Parker that uses the shadows of hundreds of thousands of tiny steel pins to form black-and-white pictures; the configuration of the pins is altered before each exposure.

Pixilation A STOP-MOTION technique in which full-sized props and live actors are photographed FRAME-BY-FRAME to achieve unusual effects of motion.

Platen A sheet of heavy glass used to hold cels flat and still during shooting. The use of the platen also prevents shadows from the painted areas from falling on the BACKGROUND.

Plot 1) To plan and calibrate the movements of the artwork and/or camera for PANS, TRUCKS, and ROTATIONS. 2) The story line of a film.

Pose-To-Pose Animation A method of animation in which the animator plans the movements in advance, enabling him to draw the EXTREMES, and the ASSISTANT ANIMATOR to draw the IN-BETWEENS; as opposed to straight-ahead animation. Pose-to-pose is the method commonly used in STUDIO ANIMATION.

Postproduction The work done on a film once photography has been completed, such as EDITING, developing and printing, LOOPING, etc.

Producer In STUDIO ANIMATION, the administrative head of the film, usually responsible for budget, staff, legal contracts, distribution, scheduling, etc.

Production Supervisor In STUDIO ANIMATION, an assistant to the PRODUCER, in charge of routine administrative duties.

Projection Speed The rate at which the film moves through the projector; twenty-four frames per second is the standard for all sound films.

Punch The device that cuts the REGISTRATION holes in cels and drawing paper, so they can be placed over the corresponding PEGS.

Puppet Animation An animation technique in which three-dimensional articulated figures are manipulated on miniature SETS and photographed FRAME-BY-FRAME.

Rackover A method of checking the precise center of the camera's field, in which the body of the camera is temporarily shifted to one side to allow the CAMERA OPERATOR to look through a special viewfinder with cross hairs; the camera is shifted back into position for shooting to continue. Rackovers are often used to check the accuracy of off-center shots.

Raw Stock Film that has not been exposed or processed.

Registration The exact alignment of the various pieces of artwork in relation to each other, made possible in animation by the use of the PEG system.

Release Print See COMPOSITE PRINT.

Rotation A camera move in which the camera is moved in a complete circle to give a spinning effect in the film. A partial rotation is called a Tilt.

Rotoscope A device patented by Max Fleischer in 1917, that projects live-action film, one frame at a time, onto a small screen from the rear. Drawing paper is placed over the screen allowing the animators to trace the live-action images as a guide in capturing complicated movements.

Roughs The animators' original drawings, which are usually broad and sketchy, rather than finished drawings, and which are refined by the CLEANUP Artist.

Saturday Morning Television A term which has its roots in the child-oriented, LIMITED ANIMATION cartoon shows that began to dominate this time slot in the 1950's, but has come to stand for this genre of mass-produced animation.

Scene A segment of a film that depicts a single situation or incident.

Scene Planner In STUDIO ANIMATION, the person who works with the DIRECTOR and STORYBOARD artist to do detailed drawings of the scene, indicating the PATH OF ACTION, background elements, camera moves, etc. Also known as a Layout Artist. See LAYOUT.

Script The text of a film, giving dialogue, action, staging, camera moves, etc.

Set Derived from "setting." The prepared stage on which the action for three-dimensional animation takes place. A set may be as simple as a plain tabletop, or as elaborate as props and decoration can make it.

Sequence A group of related SCENES in a film that combine to tell a particular portion of the story, and which are usually set in the same location or time span.

Short The term usually refers to the cartoons made in the Hollywood studios during the 1930's, 1940's, and 1950's, which ran between 6 and 7 minutes long. Today, shorts range from one and one-half to over 20 minutes in length and cover a variety of styles and subjects.

Shot An unbroken filmed segment; the basic component of a SCENE.

Show Reel A sample reel of film of an animator's work, used as a portfolio in obtaining jobs.

Silhouette Animation A type of cutout animation in which only the shapes of the figures are shown against a BACKGROUND; brought to its highest development by Lotte Reiniger.

Slow In/Slow Out Refers to the fact that PANNING and TRUCKING moves usually begin slowly, gradually attain their full speed, then slow to a stop, to avoid a sense of jerkiness in the movement.

Sound The audio portion of a film, which consists of three components: music, sound effects, and voices (either DIALOGUE or NARRATION).

Splice The joining together of two pieces of film—either photographic or magnetic; the join is made with cement or splicing tape.

Squash and Stretch An element of CHARACTER ANIMATION which involves the exaggeration of the normal tendency of an object in motion to undergo a degree of distortion, lengthening as it travels, and compressing as it stops.

Staging The planning of how the action will take place.

Stand The entire photographing unit, including the COMPOUND, camera, and CRANE.

Standard Field See FIELD.

Stop Motion The animation of three-dimensional objects by moving them slightly before each exposure; used extensively in monster movies to bring imaginary creatures to life. Also called Stop Action.

Storyboard A series of small consecutive drawings with accompanying caption-like descriptions of the action and sound, which are arranged comic-strip fashion and used to plan a film. The drawings are frequently tacked to corkboards so that individual drawings can be added or changed in the course of development. Invented at the Disney studio, the technique is now widely used for live-action films and commercials, as well as animation.

Studio Animation Animation characterized by the fact that the various aspects of production are done by different people and, in the case of larger studios, different departments; the finished product is the result of a coordinated group effort.

Synchronization The coordination of the sound and picture, so they are matched precisely in the finished film; also referred to as Sync.

Take A reaction by a character. Tex Avery was famous for his use of wildly extreme takes in his films: eyes would bulge to the size of watermelons, jaws would drop and knock holes through tables, tongues would unroll to several feet, etc.

Thaumatrope An early animation device that consisted of a disc with one image painted on each side; when the disc was spun on a loop of string, the images seemed to appear together.

Timing A LABORATORY process that involves balancing the color of a film to achieve consistency from scene to scene. Also includes adjusting exposure settings in duplication.

Traveling Peg Bars See PANNING PEG BARS.

Truck A camera move in which the camera seems to move toward (Truck In) or away

from (Truck Out) the subject. The same effect is called a zoom in live-action filmmaking.

Underlighting See BOTTOM LIGHTING.

Video Animation Stand A special unit designed to photograph animation on videotape. The recorder moves the tape in one twenty-fourth of a second increments that correspond to frames of film. Its instant replay capacity makes it useful for PENCIL TESTS.

View Finder A registration device mounted near the top of the animation STAND that allows the CAMERA OPERATOR to check whether or not the camera is trained on the center of the FIELD. See RACKOVER.

Voice Artist An actor who performs the voices for the animated characters during a recording session.

Voice-Over See NARRATION.

Wipe A transition in which one scene appears to advance onto the screen over another; the leading edge may be a straight line, or it may describe a shape, such as a circle or an animated drip.

Workprint A print of the film made from the ORIGINAL for EDITING purposes. When the DIRECTOR is satisfied with the editing of the workprint, the original will be cut to match it, so that RELEASE PRINTS can be struck.

Xerography A special form of photocopying on CELS; developed by the Disney studio in conjunction with the Xerox Corporation. Used instead of inking to transfer the animation drawings onto CELS.

Zoetrope An early animation device that uses strips of sequential drawings that are spun and viewed through slits in a rotating drum to create an illusion of motion.

Zoom See TRUCK.

Index